Letts Study Aids

History 1

Foundation Skills for 11-14 year olds

Martin L. Parsons BA

Deputy Head of Lower School,
Head of Lower School Humanities,
Theale Green Comprehensive

Charles Letts & Co Ltd
London, Edinburgh & New York

First published 1986
by Charles Letts & Co Ltd
Diary House, Borough Road, London SE1 1DW

Illustrations: Peter McClure

© Martin L Parsons 1986

All our Rights Reserved. No part of this publication may be reproduced, stored in a retrieval system, or transmitted, in any form or by any means, electronic, mechanical, photo-copying, recording or otherwise, without the prior permission of Charles Letts Publishers

ISBN 0 85097 654 5

Printed in Great Britain by
Charles Letts (Scotland) Ltd

Acknowledgements

The Controller of Her Majesty's Stationery Office, for permission to reproduce examples of Birth and Death Certificates and Identity card. The Tithe Barn Museum, Swanage, for providing and allowing the reproduction of archive photographs relating to the Stone Quarrying Industry.
J A S Green MA, Berkshire County Archivist, for documents relating to Units 22 and 23.
C Parsons BLib, Oxfordshire Schools Library Service, for information relating to Units 35 and 36.
D F Skilton Esq., Company Secretary of Huntley Boorne & Stevens Ltd., for permission to reproduce archive photographs and documents.
N Crompton Esq., History Projects Officer of the Fire Service Society, for permission to reproduce archive photographs and documents.
P Cox Esq., 'Fotosparks' Reading, for technical assistance with photographic material.
The Parsons and Brown families for permitting the reproduction of personal documents.
G T Lilley Esq., for permission to reproduce his letter.
B Griffin Esq., for academic advice and assistance.
Museum of English Rural Life, Reading – for permission to take photographs for Unit 37.
Mrs D Pritchard
Berkshire Group of newspapers for permission to reproduce newspaper articles in Unit 35.
A & C Black for permission to reproduce extracts from *A School Edition of the Diary of Samuel Pepys*, Editor C J Hall, 1924

References

A Dictionary of Modern History 1789–1945, A W Palmer, Penguin 1979
Archives of the Reading Volunteer Fire Brigade
A School Edition of the Diary of Samuel Pepys, Editor C J Hall, A & C Black, 1924
Curiosities of Swanage, David Lewer and J Bernard Calkin, Friary Press 1971
English Domestic Architecture, A L Osborne, Country Life 1967
Keesings Contemporary Archives
The Berkshire County Record Office Index
The Bollard Story, Sidney Tringham
What is History? Jon Nichol, Blackwell 1981
Yattendon for Visitors, R G Greenaway

The authors and publishers are grateful to the following organizations and individuals for permitting us to reproduce photographs and illustrations for which they hold the copyright:

Aerofilms Library: p. 88; All Action Photographic: pp. 10, 22; BBC Hulton Picture Library: pp. 12, 13, 17, 19, 26, 67;
Derek G Widdicombe/Countrywide Photographic Library: p. 80; Mary Evans Picture Library: pp. 61, 62; Pam Isherwood/Format: p. 98;
N. Holland: p. 81; Imperial War Museum: pp. 53, 54; National Portrait Gallery, London: pp. 19, 26, 36, 37, 58; Syndication International: p. 10

Preface

History is an important part of the curriculum for young people between the ages of 10 and 14. Not only does it give pupils an appreciation of their heritage, it also allows the development of skills involved in the individual interpretation of available facts and evidence.

In some schools history is taught as a separate subject discipline, while in other schools it may form part of a Humanities or Environmental Studies course. However, in whatever guise it is taught, the approach to the subject should be similar, and the material used should provide sufficient stimulus to motivate pupils into seeking more knowledge and questioning what they see around them in their environment.

Foundation Skills: History, Volumes 1–3 is a group of books designed not only to introduce young people to history, but also to acquaint them with the simple skills and methods which will help them study the subject in a more interesting way.

History should be a fascinating and enjoyable subject, but, unfortunately, too many young people are put off by the belief that history is only a study of dates, and often by the adverse comments of adults for whom this style of history was the only one they received at school. Nothing could be further from the truth. Over the past few years there has been a strong move towards the **'investigative'** study of history. It is no longer necessary to learn a lot of dates or put events into a sequential order just for the sake of doing so. Facts and clues now need to be gathered and assimilated to provide the basis of an historical study, therefore the historian needs to be a detective, and the young historian can consider any investigation as a form of treasure hunt with the final answer, or theory, being the treasure. In order to find the required information and use it properly, the young historian needs to acquire certain concepts and ideas, and master specific skills. Some of these skills are very simple and require little thought and effort, but others need to be developed over a period of time, gradually increasing in complexity, and mastered in sequence. By following Volumes 1–3 the pupil will be able to experience these skills and, eventually, in Volume 3, put them into practical use in the production of his or her own individual historical project.

The series will provide not only a concise explanation of the skills, but also a large number of exercises which will be used to reinforce the issues raised in the text. Some of these may be in the form of simple questions and answers, or comprehension exercises involving the text or other stimulus material, or involve the physical search for evidence. Others will require the young person to explore beyond the immediate environment of his or her home and to look more closely at the local community. In all cases parental help will be very important. If all the exercises are completed and all the suggestions in the **Activities** sections are followed up, the child will have a more than sufficient foundation for continuing with the subject at 16+.

This series of books has involved a great deal of research in all aspects of the subject. My general acknowledgements are listed, but I must thank Brian Griffin for all his constructive criticism and support, the staff of Charles Letts & Co Ltd for their help and guidance, Peter Cox of 'Fotosparks' Reading, for his expert photographic advice and Dianne Pritchard for her supreme patience.

Also I must thank my wife Josephine and my daughters Kimiko and Hannah for their continued understanding and support.

Introduction
and guide to using this book

In the past many schools have taught the subject of History to 11 to 14 year olds by the simple method of 'Text-book, notes and illustrations'. Although taking notes from a text is an important skill, it can become boring and counter-productive if it is used continually. The gradual move away from this style of teaching towards 'investigative' history study has allowed young people to discover history for themselves and to develop skills which will make them less reliant on other people's work and more on their own investigations and deductions.

This series of books covers the skills necessary for such investigation and is designed to help the pupil develop his or her own techniques. The three volumes are aimed at the 11 to 14 age group and the content increases in difficulty from the simple text and exercises in Volume 1, to the writing of a structured history project in Volume 3.

Volume 1: (primarily for 10/11 to 12 year olds and those for whom History is a new subject) looks at the very basic skills required by any historian and starts to investigate simple ways in which one or more of them can be used to help answer a specific question or support a specific theory.

Volume 2: (for 12 to 13 year olds) develops some of the skills in Volume 1 to a greater level of understanding, and introduces new skills and methods.

Volume 3: (for 13 to 14 year olds) takes the skills learned in Volumes 1 and 2 and develops them in more practical terms by way of a structured local and/or family project. This volume also looks at the topic of essay work and the different types of examination questions a pupil is likely to see in school and external examinations. Reference will also be made to how this subject may help in future careers.

By working through the three volumes in sequence, the pupil, and parents, should gain a fuller understanding of the investigative skills required in this subject, and the pupil at the age of fourteen will be in a better position to decide whether or not to continue with History at external examination level.

To help understand the structure of the books there is a **Skills/Concepts Analysis** chart on page 8. Down the left-hand side of the page are listed the skills required by any historian, and across the top are the general **Unit/Topic** headings. The numbers 1, 2, 3, in the boxes refer to the volume in which that particular skill is covered. You will notice that some of the topics are covered in all three volumes, in varying degrees of complexity, hence the use of all three numbers in some of the boxes. You will see that the full range of skills will not be covered unless the full course is followed. The topics should be studied in the same order as they appear in the volumes, but reference will be made in Volumes 2 and 3 to topics covered in previous volumes. Much of the work in Volume 3 cannot be understood without first learning the basic requirements investigated in Volumes 1 and 2.

Almost all the units have exercises in an **Activities** section and they should all be attempted in order to reinforce the skills and methods covered in the text. Some units require more detailed explanation than others, so may not have space available for a specific Activities section related to it. However, at intervals in the book there are **Revision Units** which will provide questions and exercises on the work studied in a number of units dealing with the same topic. Some of the exercises need a simple written answer, but others require the pupil to investigate his or her own environment. All the answers to those questions needing them will be found in the **Answers** section which starts on page 124. There is also a glossary of words which the pupil may find difficult to understand in the text.

Finally, my apologies to all female would-be historians: for the purpose of simplicity and consistency I have had to refer to the historian as 'he' throughout.

These books are written with the pupil in mind and are designed to make the study of history an enjoyable and rewarding experience.

Contents

Preface   3

Introduction and guide to using this book   5

Topic and skills analysis table   8

Unit 1   What is History?
Answers the questions What is history? When does history start? When do we refer to it and use History, sometimes without realizing it?   10

Unit 2   Personal time scale
The reader in his or her own historical time. An awareness of personal history and how it can be illustrated.   12

Unit 3   Historical time scale
The reader in relation to the national or world events they have lived through.   14

Unit 4   Family time scale
The reader's family history, and how this history can be illustrated.   16

Unit 5   British historical events
Introduction to some historical events throughout the family time scale. An introduction to the very simple use of tables and charts.   19

Unit 6   Measurement of time
The measurement of time. The understanding of BC and AD. The numbering of centuries and certain key facts to aid the student's awareness of time.   22

Unit 7   People in pictures
History is about people in the past, some easily recognizable from pictures or written descriptions, others not. This unit sets out to extract information from pictures and shows how the information can be used by the historian.   26

Unit 8   People in written sources
This unit extracts information from written sources and shows how this information can be used by the historian.   28

Unit 9   Crafts and trades
What people did to earn a living can give us a clue to life and conditions in the past. This unit uses simple written material and illustrates how clues to the past can be extracted.   30

Revision unit
Search for words and clues used in Units 1 to 9   32

Unit 10   Detection: A local area
This unit provides evidence from a local area from which facts can be easily extracted. It also explains simply the use of Latin numbers.   33

Unit 11   Detection: Connections
A simple exercise to find the 'common factor' between different sources of information.   36

Unit 12   Detection: a combination of sources
An explanation of how the common link between a number of sources can provide information which will lead to an answer to a question.   40

Revision Unit: Treasure trail
An exercise where certain clues need to be read carefully and put into their correct sequence in order to make up a story.   42

Unit 13   Problem of evidence
This unit explains how too much, as well as too little, evidence can alter opinion. The reader will see how to make a choice between various items in order to make a decision. Simple discrimination.   43

Unit 14   Cause and effect
Using the example of early man this unit investigates the reasons for the development of his tools and weapons.   46

Unit 15   Primary sources
What are primary sources and how can they be used? This unit provides and explains different examples of primary source material. It also introduces the subject of bias.   48

Unit 16   The use of photographs
Photographs have already been used in this book but what do they show us? This unit explains that there can be a difference between what the photographer wants the viewer to see and what he actually sees.   50

Unit 17   Photographs: care in use
What to be wary of when using any photograph.   52

Revision Units 16 and 17
The extraction of simple historical facts from a series of photographs.   55

Unit 18 Diaries
How diaries can be useful sources while remembering that their contents are only one person's point of view. 57

Unit 19 The diary of Samuel Pepys
Extracts from Pepys' diaries as examples of how useful such sources can be. 60

Unit 20 Letters
Letters as a source of information; but what to remember when using them. 64

Unit 21 Letters in newspapers
This unit uses an original letter, extracts information from it, and discusses just how useful such letters can be. 66

Unit 22 Personal records and documents
The extraction of simple clues from personal documentation including marriage, birth and death certificates, ration cards, identity cards and school reports. 68

Unit 23 The search for documents and records
This unit provides step-by-step information on how to find a required document from a county records' office. 73

Unit 24 Place names
A clue to the possible beginnings of a village or town can be found in its name. 76

Unit 25 Introduction to building styles
A look at some of the reasons why buildings and building materials have changed throughout history. 80

Unit 26 Building styles up to 1500s
The clues to look for when dating buildings before the Tudor Age. 82

Unit 27 Building styles 1700 to 1910
The clues to look for when dating buildings from the Georgian to Edwardian periods. 84

Unit 28 Building styles, 20th century
The clues to look for when dating buildings from the 20th century. 88

Revision Units 25 to 28
A series of questions and exercises dealing with information provided in Units 25 to 28. 91

Unit 29 Introduction to artefacts
How articles from the past can help the historian. How they can be dated. 92

Unit 30 More about artefacts
How to examine articles and gather simple information about them. What questions to ask yourself about them and how to start your own index card file on any articles which interest you. 95

Unit 31 Collecting artefacts: an historical hobby
How collecting artefacts can become a worthwhile historical hobby. 98

Unit 32 Secondary sources
What are secondary sources? This unit provides and explains different examples of secondary source material which will be discussed in subsequent units and volumes 2 and 3. 102

Unit 33 Libraries
Libraries are very useful to the historian. This unit explains how to locate the books you may require in a library; how to use the library catalogue, the Dewey Classification system, and shows the importance of a book's 'Contents' and 'Index'. 104

Unit 34 History books
The use of history books as a source of information. 108

Unit 35 Local newspapers
How useful are local newspapers as a source of historical information? Where do you find them and how do you extract relevant facts from them? 110

Revision Unit: Local newspapers
A comprehension exercise using a genuine newspaper article as a source. 114

Unit 36 National newspapers
How national newspapers differ from local ones. Why the information contained in them sometimes needs to be used with care. 116

Unit 37 Museums
A simple guide to using museums with a brief description of the different types. 118

Unit 38 Sources
A diagrammatic summary of historical sources. 121

Answers 124

Glossary 128

SKILLS \ TOPICS	What is History?	Personal time scale	Family time scale	Historical time scale	People – Characters	Crafts and trades	Detection: use of evidence	Problem of evidence	Cause and effect	Primary sources Introduction	Use of photographs	Diaries and letters	Documents	Place names	Buildings/architecture	Artefacts	Secondary sources Introduction	History books
NOTE-TAKING																		
Simple: single source	1	1	1	1	1	1	1	1	1	1	1	1	1	1	1	1	1	1
Specific: more than one source							1/2/3	1/2/3	1			2			1/2/3	1/2/3		1/2/3
Variety: many sources					3		1/2/3	1/2/3			3	3			1/2/3	3		1/2/3
LITERACY																		
Comprehension – clear text	1	1	1	1	1	1	1	1	1	1	1	1	1	1	1	1	1	1
Use of index							1				1							1
Use of library				1				1	1		1	1	1	1	1	1		1
Ability to answer in sentences		1	1	1	1		1	1	1		2	2		1		2		2
Comprehension – demanding text			3		3	3	3		3		2/3	2/3			3			3
Ability to answer in paragraphs			3		3	3			3		3	3	3	3	3	3		3
More imaginative writing																		
Comprehension – complex material																		3
Project work			3		3	3					3	3		3	3	3		
Factual essays																		
Specific library study																		
Exam technique																		
HISTORICAL METHOD																		
Knowledge of primary sources Simple evaluation	1	1	1	1	1	1	1	1	1		1	1	1	1	1	1		1
More detailed sources primary and secondary				1	1				1		1	1	2/3	1	1	1		1
Simple detection of bias							1	1			1	1						1
Evaluation of complex material											3	3	3		3	3		3
Interpretation of documents			1				1					1	1/2/3					
Discrimination of material							1	1			1/2/3	1/2/3	1/2/3			1/2/3		1/2/3
HISTORICAL UNDERSTANDING																		
Simple accounts in context		1	1		1	1	1	1	1							1		1
Defending views of historical character					1							1						
Written answers from more than one viewpoint																		
SENSE OF TIME																		
Feel for time	1	1	1	1	1	1		1			1	1		1	1	1		1
Lines of development		1	1	1			1		1				1	1	1	1/2		
Sequential aids to overall knowledge		1	1	1											1			

Libraries and museums	Sources	Note-taking	Précis	Interpretation of graphs and statistics	History around us	Use and interpretation of maps	Detection: village development	Accounts and lists	Personal records	Log books	Archive film	Cause and effect: villages	Choosing a project title	Planning a project	Use of libraries	Gathering material	Evaluation of material	Illustrations	Project examples	Using the essay title	Planning the essay	Using many sources	Writing the essay	Exam: preparation and revision	Multi-choice exams	Exam essays	Further historical study	Reading list
1	1	2	2	2	2	2	2	2	2	2	2	2	3	3	3	3	3	3	3	3	3	3	3	3	3	3	3	3
		2	2	2	2	2	2	2	2	2	2	2	3	3	3	3	3	3	3	3	3		3	3	3			
3		2		2	2	2	2	2				2	3			3	3	3			3	3					3	3
1	1	2	2	2	2	2	2	2	2	2	2	2	3	3	3	3	3	3	3	3	3	3	3	3	3	3	3	3
1						2	2									3						3						
1	1				2	2			2		2				1/2/3	3												3
		2	2	2	2	2	2	2	2	2	2	2				3		3		3		3					
		3	2/3	3		2	3					2				3	3	3	3		3		3		3		
			2	2			2					2										3					
			2			2	2					2				3		3				3					
				2					2							3		3				3			3		
3		3	3	3	3	3	2/3	3		3	3	3	2	3	3	3	3	3	3								3	3
																			3	3	3	3				3		
1													3		3			3		3	3						3	
																							3	3	3	3		
	1	2	2	2	2	2	2	2	2	2	2	2	3			3	3	3		3	3	3			3		
		2		2	2	2/3	2	2	2	2	2	2	3	3	3	3								3			
				2/3		2		2	2		2					3	3	3			3							
				3	3	3		3	3		3					3		3		3	3			3	3			
1		2	2	2/3	2/3	2/3	2	2/3	2/3	2		2	3	3		3		3			3			3				
			2/3	2/3	2/3	2/3	2/3	2/3	2/3	2/3		2/3				3	3	3	3	3	3		3		3			
					2	2	2					2				3		3			3				3			
								2	2	2						3				3	3				3			
																3				3	3				3			
		2		2/3	2/3	2		2		2	2/3					3		3			3			3				
	1				2/3	2					2/3					3					3	3	3					
	1				2						2					3					3			3				

Unit 1

What is History?

history (*his-to-ri*) n. the study of the past or past events; a record of events in the life of a nation, state, institution etc.

If you look up the word 'history' in a dictionary it will say something similar to the extract above, that **'history is the study of the past or past events'**.

You may not have known what history was, but you have probably studied it at school or even at home without realizing it. You may call it Environmental Studies or Humanities, but whenever you ask someone a question about the past, you are asking about history.

Who won the F.A. Cup Final in 1983? (The picture on the right may give you a clue.) Which popsinger had a number one hit with a song about the First World War, in January 1984? These are very simple historical questions. They are asking about things that have happened in the past. But they are the sort of questions you might ask or discuss with a friend at any time.

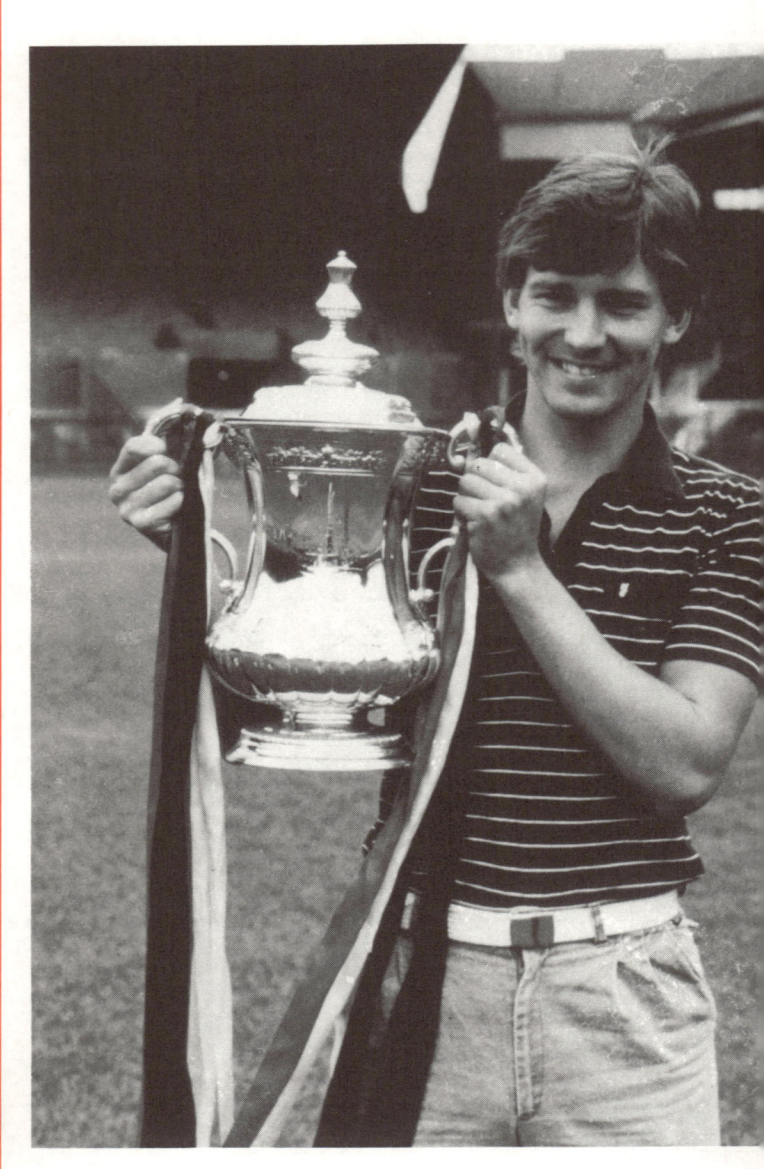

1.1 When does history begin?

But if history is the study of the past, or past events, when does history start? You may say 'When the world began' or 'At the beginning of time', both reasonable answers. But think very carefully; if history is the study of the past when did the past begin? Write down on a piece of paper your name, the date, and the time you had breakfast e.g. James Smith, Monday 4 Jan 1984, Breakfast: 7.10 a.m. Now write down what you had for breakfast e.g. cereal, toast, coffee. Will you have cereal, toast, coffee at 7.10 a.m. on Monday 4 Jan 1984 again? The answer is 'no' because it is now in the past, the time has gone, it is history. So did history start at breakfast time? Look at your watch or clock, and write down the time and date e.g. 10.30 a.m. 4 January 1984. By the time you have finished writing it, 10.30 or whatever time you wrote down, will have passed, it has become . . . history.

Therefore, when does history start? In fact, it starts **now**, because as soon as you say or do something it has gone and will not return at exactly the same time again, it becomes history.

1.2 What is history about?

Unfortunately the study of history is not as simple as the example we have used here. It is a study of all the things from, and to do with the past: people, events, articles, buildings, documents, pictures and many other things besides. However, this book, and the two that follow it, will help you study the subject in an organized and enjoyable way. It will deal with the skills the historian needs, but will not necessarily use the topics or material you are studying at school. This does not matter because the skills you learn from this book will help you with any historical topic and in other subjects as well.

Activities

Most of the exercises for this and other units can be done at home, but some will make you look around at your surroundings or environment and search for historical clues. When you reach Volume 3 you should have enough experience of basic skills to undertake your own historical project. History is a fascinating and enjoyable subject and I hope the text and exercises will help you understand it better and build up your historical knowledge.

We can start with a basic skill required by all historians at all levels of experience, the ability to read a passage and pick out simple information from it. I suggest you read through this unit again and then answer the questions below. All the answers can be found in the text, and you can check them in the Answers section on page 124.

1. When does history start?
2. Which word in the text means 'surroundings'?
3. In which book should you look up the word history?
4. What name was used in the example?
5. Write down the exact time that the person in the example had breakfast.
6. What did he have for breakfast?

More Activities

Look at this book, the cover and the first few pages before this unit, and see how observant you are. Answer these questions; they will require a little more searching.

(a) Which publisher is responsible for producing this series of books?
(b) Who is the author?
(c) What do the letters BA after his name stand for?
(d) What date was this book first published?
(e) Where was this book printed?

Summary

1. History is the study of everything and everybody in the past.
2. History starts now.
3. One of the basic skills the history student must have is the ability to pick out information from a passage of writing.

Unit 2

Personal time scale

The easiest way to start a study of history is with yourself. You have lived through a number of years, according to your age, and many things have happened in that time. You may have had your tonsils taken out or you may have had a special holiday. These and many other events are part of your personal history, and although they may not have had any effect on world affairs, they make up an important part of that stage of your life which is in the past.

2.1 Sources of information

Some of the events you can easily remember because they occurred recently, but some you will not remember because they happened a long time ago. In order to find out about these distant times you will have to use another basic historical skill, that of putting questions to a source who knows the answer. The source of information in this case is, of course, those people who have known you all your life: your parents, grandparents and relatives. They will tell you stories about yourself which you may not wish to hear, but they can also give you some very useful information about yourself. You may not think this is history, but it certainly is!

Some parents keep a 'Baby Book'. This may be a proper book with your height and weight recorded at different stages of your early life, sometimes they also include photographs. Or it may be a scrap-book in which your parents have kept the newspaper cuttings announcing your birth, your hospital tag, congratulations cards and telegrams from friends and relatives, and many other such things.

Activities

Ask your parents if they have such a book or a collection of **memorabilia**. If they have, look at it carefully, it will give you some useful information. While you are reading through this material write down on the page of a notebook all those facts you find particularly interesting.

You can do this according to the year or your age. Put your name at the top of the page and lay it out as follows:

Either

Fig. 2.1

> JOHN. Born 1974
>
> 1974 Born Monday, 11th November 6.30 p.m.
> 1975 May. Began to crawl
> 1976 Feb. Walked for the first time.

or

> JOHN. Born 1974
>
> AGE 0–1 Born Monday 11th. Nov. 6.30 p.m.
> 6 months – Began to crawl.
> AGE 1–2
> 15 months – Walked for the first time.

Do not forget you also need to include the events that your relatives have told you about. You may wish to leave out the humorous or embarrassing events or others which you do not consider important. You need to try to sort out those events which actually happened from those which might have happened. You will have to be careful of answers similar to 'When you were four you fell down the stairs. Well, I think it was you. Or was it your sister?' It is not clear who actually fell down the stairs and if you are not sure you should not use the information. However, in this example, how could you find out for certain who actually fell? (Write down your answer and check it in the Answers section on page 124.)

When you have gathered your information from the scrap book and from asking questions of your relatives, how do you present it?

Presenting the information

If you have found a good collection of photographs of yourself at various ages you may be able to use them to display your life so far. Stick them on to a large piece of paper in date order and clearly label each photograph. (See Fig. 2.2.) By doing it this way you gain a clear pictorial or **visual** arrangement of your history, but, of course, unless you are very lucky there will be gaps. Another way is to write down your historical time-line. You can either start at the present year and work backwards or start at the year you were born and work forwards. Using this method you can include all the information you have collected. Take a sheet of paper, mark the years on the left-hand side of the page. Do not forget to leave plenty of space between each year to allow for all the information you have previously written down in rough; for example: 1974 Born 11 Nov Grandma came to stay.

Given a teddy by Uncle Tom.

Complete each year until you reach the present day. Some years may have more entries than others, so it may be better to write down each year heading only when you have finished the previous one.

Now you have two ways of presenting your life. Why not use the two together? Use the photographs where possible, and where you have gaps write down the information for that time. (The photographs may require some writing to explain them.)

If you do this on poster-size paper it would look rather impressive on your bedroom wall. The neater you present your material the easier it will be to read and get facts from later on.

Fig. 2.2

Summary

1 You are a part of history and like everyone else you have a personal history.

2 Studying your own history is the simplest way to experience some of the basic skills required by the historian.

3 In this unit we have seen:

(**a**) the need to ask questions when there is a gap in your knowledge;
(**b**) the need to think carefully about the information you receive. In this case you need to consider whether the answers to your questions are accurate. If there is any doubt, you need to ask somebody else who knows about the same event and see if their answer agrees or disagrees with the first one;
(**c**) the need to have a notebook with you at all times to record your facts;
(**d**) the need to present your material in a neat and interesting way.

4 An historian requires patience to search for and look through as much material as possible, knowing that possibly not all of it will be used.

Unit 3
Historical time scale

In Unit 2 we looked at your personal history; at the events that you have taken an active part in, or which have concerned you in other ways during your lifetime. In this unit we are going to look at the history you have lived through, which has not directly affected you personally.

We could do this in many ways. If you are interested in 'pop' music you may like to make a list of all the Number 1 hits during your life, or if you are interested in sport you could make a list of all the F.A. Cup Winners, or the league champions during the same period. This may not seem to you to be an historical study, but it is, because these events have all happened in the past and are therefore history.

You can use many other interests and make a **chronological** list of this kind, of course you do not need to remember, or memorize all the facts on these lists, simply use them as a reference. For our example we are going to deal with the main historical events that have occurred between the years 1974 and the present day. As in Unit 2 some of the events you may be able to remember because they happened very recently, and although you could question people to find out about those that happened long ago, it may be easier to find the information you need from books.

3.1 Sources of information

Where, and how do you find the information? To make things easier we will list only those events that happened in the United Kingdom during our time-span. Sometimes you may find historical details in the back of a diary, especially if you have a specialist one like a Schoolgirls or Schoolboys. If you have not got such a list then you will need to search in an encyclopaedia or a yearly journal. Your nearest public library or your school library may have a set of these journals. They are issued every week and are bound to form a book. Look in the reference section of the library. You can easily find the year you require because each volume has a year printed on its spine. They contain a great deal of interesting historical detail for each day of the particular year covered. (When we use a book of this kind, where we can find the facts required, we are using secondary source material. This will be fully explained in Unit 32.)

3.2 Selecting the information

Before you search these books, ask questions of people and find out as much as you can about each individual year. You need to decide on the particular topic you wish to pursue, otherwise your completed chart with many different events for each year, will be complicated and confusing. For our example we will use the **political** events during our period. However, whichever topic you choose to do, do not throw away the other material because you can use it at a later date or even do more than one final chart.

3.3 Presenting the information

You now need to present your facts in such a way as to get as much information down on paper while at the same time making it easy to understand. In other words if you require a fact from your chart in a few days time you need to be able to find it quickly.

Activities

Here is a suggestion. First of all when you are noting down the facts for each year make sure you put the correct date alongside them; this will save you a lot of time later on. Taking notes for this exercise is very simple. All you need is your notebook and your pen or pencil, and as you read the book or journal write down only those facts that interest you. For example if you have chosen F.A. Cup Winners 1974 to 1985 as your topic title you do not have to write down any facts that refer to political events or royal occasions or any other subject that does not have anything to do with your title. You are sure to make mistakes in setting out your material so always do it in **rough** first, then if you do make mistakes they will not spoil the finished article.

Set out four headings on your paper as follows:

Year   Event   People involved   Outcome

Then put your **rough** notes under each heading:

Year   Event
1974   Coal Strike

When you have written down all your rough notes under the correct heading for each year you can start writing it out neatly. It may help, when doing this, to write the facts for each column in a different colour so that you can see the information at a glance. Do not forget you must put a title at the top of each page When you have finished it should look something like the example below. It shows only some of the events for one year, but it will give you an idea of the layout.

Year	Event	People Involved	Outcome
1974 9 Feb	National coal strike	HM Gov & National Union of Mine-Workers (NUM)	State of emergency 3-day working week
1974 28 Feb	General election	Edward Heath PM (Conservative) Harold Wilson (Labour) Jeremy Thorpe (Liberal)	Edward Heath resigns Harold Wilson PM
1974 6 Mar	End of coal strike	NUM	State of emergency ends
1974 24 Mar	Attempt to kidnap Princess Anne	Princess Anne Capt. Phillips	Man arrested and charged
1974 10 June	Duke of Gloucester dies	Duke of Glos	Son Richard becomes Duke
1974 10 Oct	General election	Harold Wilson PM Edward Heath Jeremy Thorpe	Labour win with increased majority

More Activities

While you are searching for information to go on to your chart, find out the answers to the following questions. They cover more than one topic, but if you have researched properly you should easily find the answers. Do not forget you can ask people who you think may know the answer, but be prepared to search through a number of books until you find the solution. (The answers to one or two may be closer than you think.)

1. Which couple won the Olympic Gold Medal in Ice Dancing at the 1984 Winter Games?
2. Which Chancellor presented his Budget to the House of Commons in March 1984?
3. Which Royal Duke died in 1947? On which date?
4. Where were the 1979 World Football Championships played?
5. What happened in London on 29 July 1981?
6. Britain was involved in a war in 1982; against whom and where was it fought?
7. There were two general elections in one year in Britain during our time scale; which year was that?
8. In 1984 England's cricketers were defeated in a Test series for the first time by one particular country. Which country?
9. Who was leader of the Conservative Party at the election in 1974?
10. Where were the 1984 Olympic Games held?

Summary

1. You have lived through historical as well as personal events.
2. Most of these events may not have affected you personally, but they have played some part in world history.
3. When doing work for a display or when taking notes, always do the work in rough first, you can make mistakes and they will not affect your finished article.
4. Remember, although we used the example of British politics, you can complete the same sort of chart for any topic that interests you.
5. Do not forget to display your work in a neat and interesting way. Use different colours for each column.

Unit 4

Family time scale

In Units 2 and 3 we looked at the two different aspects of your history – those events which affected you personally and those which, although they took place within the span of your lifetime had no direct effect on your individual life. This is a 'working' unit to help you absorb and expand the information and skills covered in Units 2 and 3.

Activities

4.1 Sources of information

We now need to expand the area of our study but we still need to keep our sources of information as simple as possible. Who, in your family, would have knowledge of the years before you were born? Your parents and grandparents have lived longer than you have so it is certain that they have a longer personal history than you. How long? Take your notebook and draw two lines at right-angles to each other, as in Fig 4.1. Along the bottom line mark off every 3 millimetres. Then, starting with 1985 at the bottom left-hand corner, write down each year at each mark i.e. 1985, 1984, 1983 etc, until you reach the end of the page. For our example we will use a family which includes a sister and brother, two parents and four grandparents. Ask the members of your family, in turn, when they were born and write down their answers; for example, Grandad Smith 1923, Grandma Smith 1927, Grandad Brown 1925, Grandma Brown 1925.

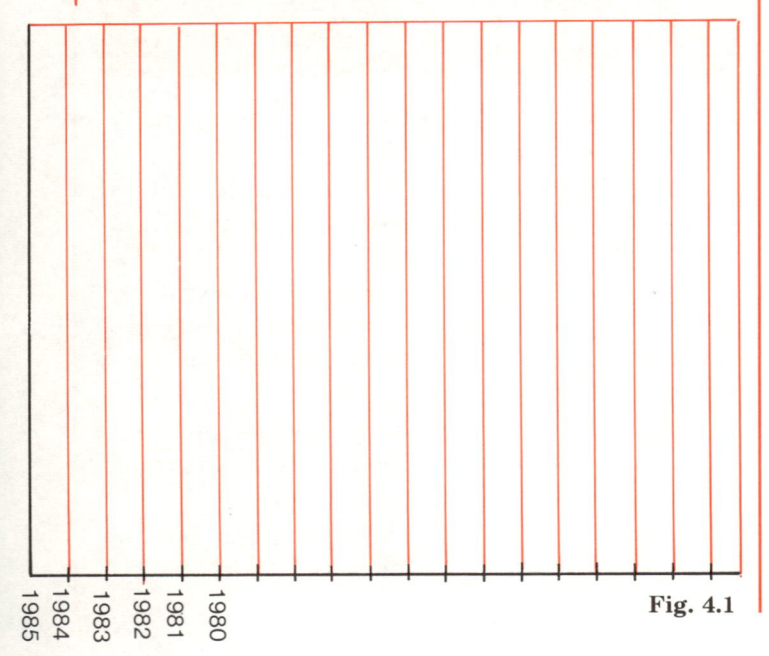

4.2 Plotting the graph

When you have asked all your family and you have the figures, plot them on your graph; start with your grandparents at the top and draw a line from the side straight out to the year they were born, see Fig. 4.2.

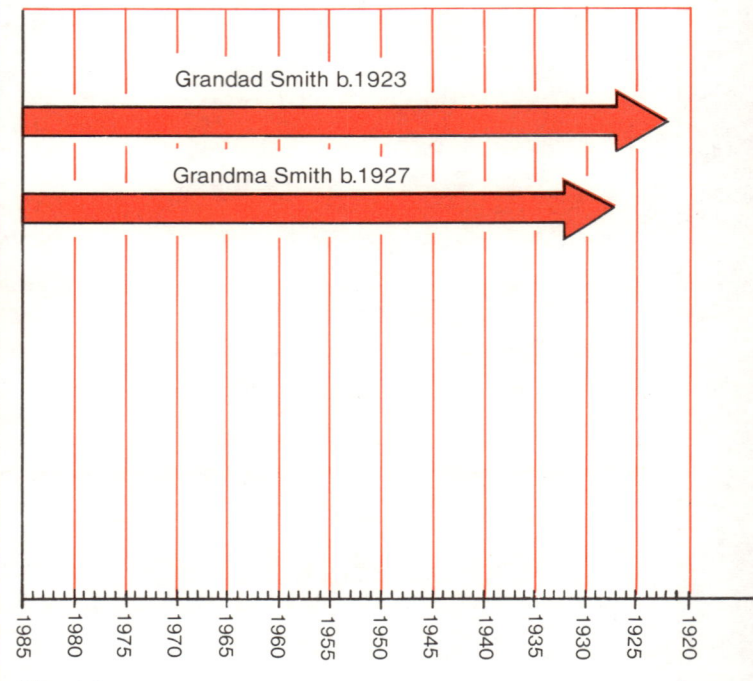

Fig. 4.2

Take each person in turn until you have a completed picture of your family's ages. You can also include your aunts and uncles, or anyone else in your family. You should now see at a glance the different life-spans each individual member of your family has had. If any of your relatives have died, you start their line in the year in which they died. For example, if your grandfather died in 1978 and was born in 1919, you would start the line in 1978 and draw it to the year 1919.

It will look better if you draw each person's life-line in a different colour, and you could put a small photograph of the individual at the end of their line. The completed drawing, using our example family, would look like Fig. 4.3.

Having plotted a simple life-line for your family you can now find out about each individual's history. The final time-line will be constructed in a way similar to your own in Unit 2, but remember it will cover more years, so your paper will need to be larger.

Fig. 4.1

Fig. 4.3

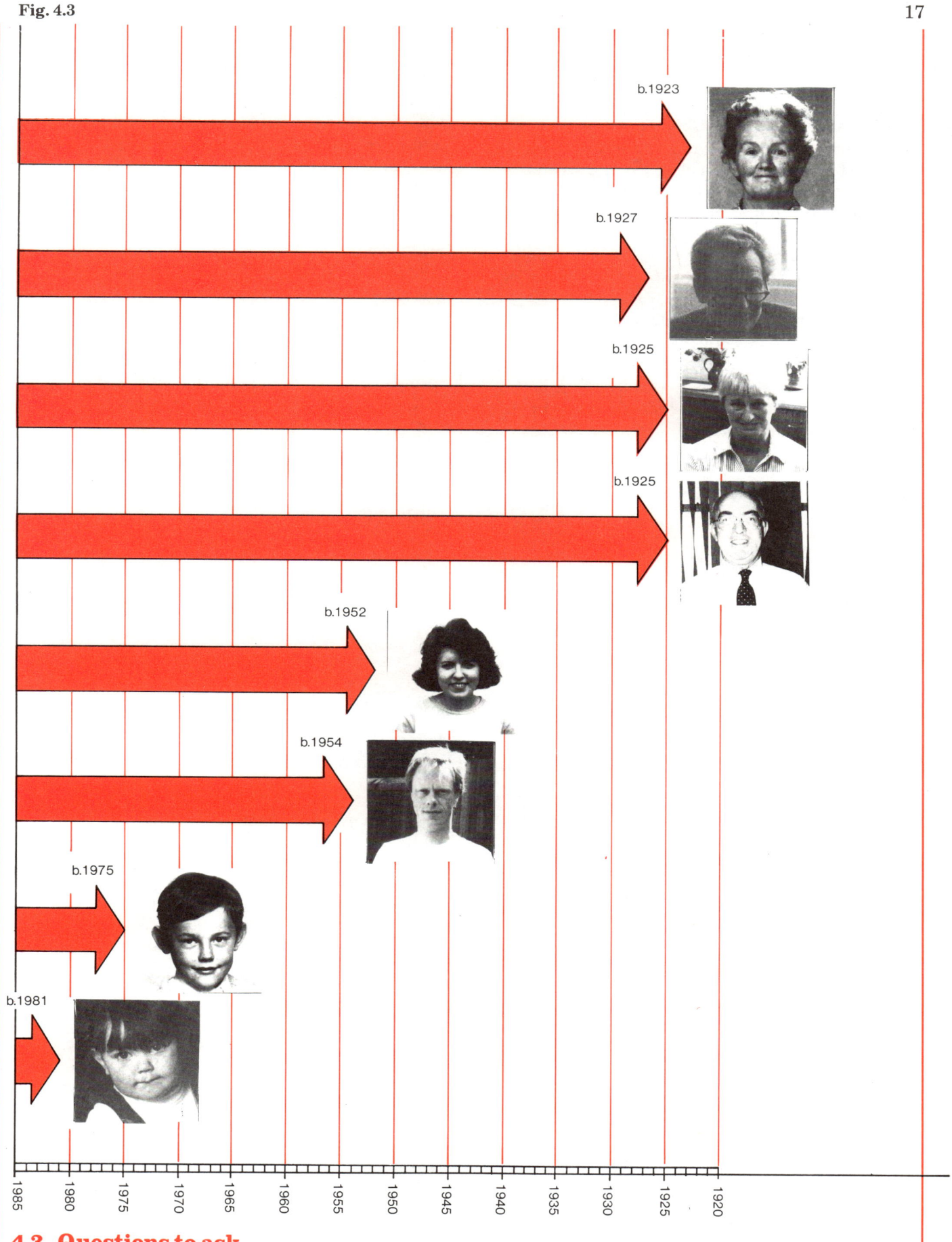

b.1923
b.1927
b.1925
b.1925
b.1952
b.1954
b.1975
b.1981

1985 1980 1975 1970 1965 1960 1955 1950 1945 1940 1935 1930 1925 1920

4.3 Questions to ask

The easiest way to find out the information for this is, of course, by asking the individuals concerned questions referring to their past. Do not forget to ask politely. You should be able to think of your own questions, but here are some suggestions to help you. You know the year they were born, but not the date, so Question 1 could

Unit 4 continued

be: When was your birthday? Question 2: Where were you born? 3: When did you first start school? 4: What was your favourite subject? 5: When did you leave school? 6: What was your first job? 7: When did you first meet grandma/grandad/dad etc? Always have your notebook ready to take down more than just the answers to your questions. You will probably find that by asking questions of this kind your parents or grandparents will remember something else that happened to them. They may not remember the year it happened, but they should have some idea of the approximate time it took place. It is better to ask each individual the same questions in order to obtain the same sort of information so that you can compare the answers. Some of the stories you may not wish to use because you may not be sure that they actually took place.

4.4 Presenting the information

When you have gathered all the material you can start writing it out. If you set out your information as follows, you can compare each person's history and at the same time immediately see their life-span.

Put a title at the top of a large sheet of squared paper, in this example 'The Personal History of the Smith Family 1923 to 1985' (write the years in the left-hand column). Start with the present year in the bottom left-hand corner and work backwards up the page. See Fig. 4.4. The space between each year will depend on the size of your paper and the number of years you have to put on it. We will use the same example family so we will need the time scales for eight people. Therefore, we will divide our page into eight columns of equal width.

Put the time scale of the oldest member of your family in the left-hand column i.e. column 1 and work towards the youngest member's time scale on the right, in this case column 7. Then start putting the information in the correct column in the space for the right year. If you can write each column in a different colour it will make it easier to see each individual's history. You now have your immediate family's history on one sheet of paper. (If you have room you can also add that of your aunts and uncles.) If you have completed all the exercises and tasks given in these first four units you should have three interesting and well-presented posters showing your personal history, an historical sequence during your life-span, and your family's personal history. All these facts should have been easy to collect, and already you are building up a very useful picture of the events that have occurred in the immediate past.

Summary

1 Your parents and grandparents have lived longer than you, therefore, they have experienced more personal events and have a longer personal history.

2 When questioning people always ask them politely. Some people may need a little persuading before they agree to answer. It will help if you explain why you need the information. Do not assume that everyone is willing to give you details of their past.

3 Sort out all your relevant information before you put it on the chart. Some of the answers may not be totally accurate.

4 When displaying your information, start with the oldest member's history in the left-hand column and work towards the youngest on the right.

5 Write the facts of each column in a different colour. (You could put a photograph of each individual at the top of their column.)

6 You should now have a good picture of your family's personal history. It can, of course, be added to as and when you find other information.

7 All the facts you have gathered so far will be very useful in Volume 3. Keep them carefully.

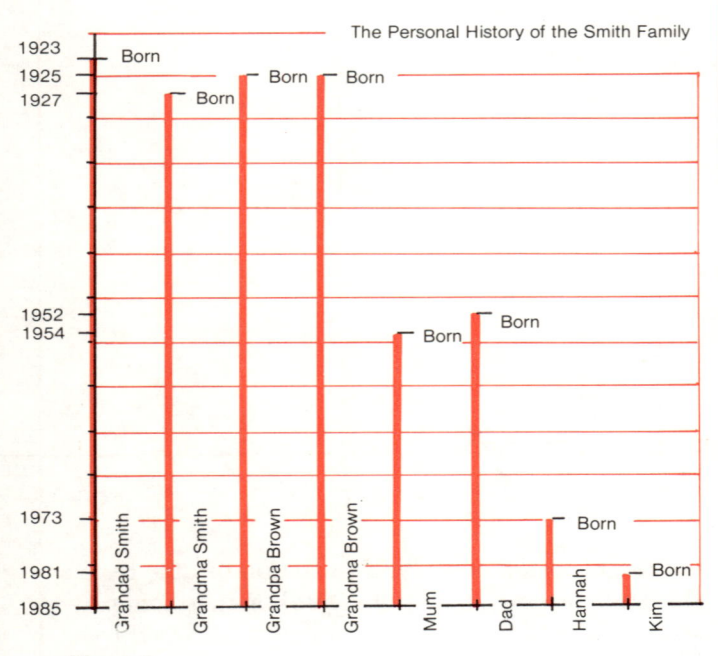

Fig. 4.4

Unit 5
British historical events

When you have completed the exercise in Unit 4 you will have a finished time-line of the personal historical facts of your immediate family. You can now complete the same exercise, this time using British historical events, to show how things have changed since your grandparents were born.

5.1 Sources of information

A basic skill required by an historian is to be able to read information in any form and understand it. So far you have been asked to find answers to questions in books and in the memories of your family. But there are other sources of information which interest and are important to the historian.

In this unit you will be given a variety of facts. Some of them will be in words and some will include numbers; two of the examples will be in pictures only. For our example we will assume that your grandparents were born in 1925, so we will limit our information from 1925 to, or near to, the present day. Each table of facts will have a title and they will be followed by a short explanation. You need to look at both very carefully, and use only those facts to answer the questions at the end of the chapter.

Date of appointment	Name	Political party
22 Jan 1924	Ramsay Macdonald	Labour
4 Nov 1925	Stanley Baldwin	Conservative
5 June 1929	Ramsay Macdonald	Labour
7 June 1935	Stanley Baldwin	Conservative
28 May 1937	Neville Chamberlain	Conservative
10 May 1940	Winston Churchill	Conservative
26 July 1945	Clement Attlee	Labour
26 Oct 1951	Sir Winston Churchill	Conservative
6 April 1955	Sir Anthony Eden	Conservative
10 Jan 1957	Harold Macmillan	Conservative
18 Oct 1963	Sir Alec Douglas-Home	Conservative
16 Oct 1964	Harold Wilson	Labour
19 June 1970	Edward Heath	Conservative
4 March 1974	Harold Wilson	Labour
5 April 1976	James Callaghan	Labour
4 May 1979	Margaret Thatcher	Conservative

Table 5.1 British Prime Ministers 1925 to 1985

Table 5.1 provides the reader with three different columns of information on a single chart. You can find out the dates on which Prime Ministers came to office since 1924, their names and the political party they represented.

Fig. 5.1 Winston Churchill

Unit 5 continued

Table 5.2 gives an idea of how much the manual workers of Britain were earning in the sample years. Note that until 1978 the women earned approximately half the wages of the men.

Year	Male	Female
1924	£2.80 (£2 16s)	£1.40 (£1 8s)
1940	£4.50 (£4 10s)	£1.90 (£1 18s)
1948	£6.90 (£6.18s)	£3.70 (£3 14s)
1960	£14.50 (£14 10s)	£7.40 (£7 8s)
1970	£26.70 (£26 14s)	£13.30 (£13 6s)
1978	£80.70	£49.40

Table 5.2 Average weekly wages for manual workers (in £.p.) in UK

Table 5.3 shows only licences issued for cars. The numbers do not include lorries, motor bicycles or other forms of motorized transport.

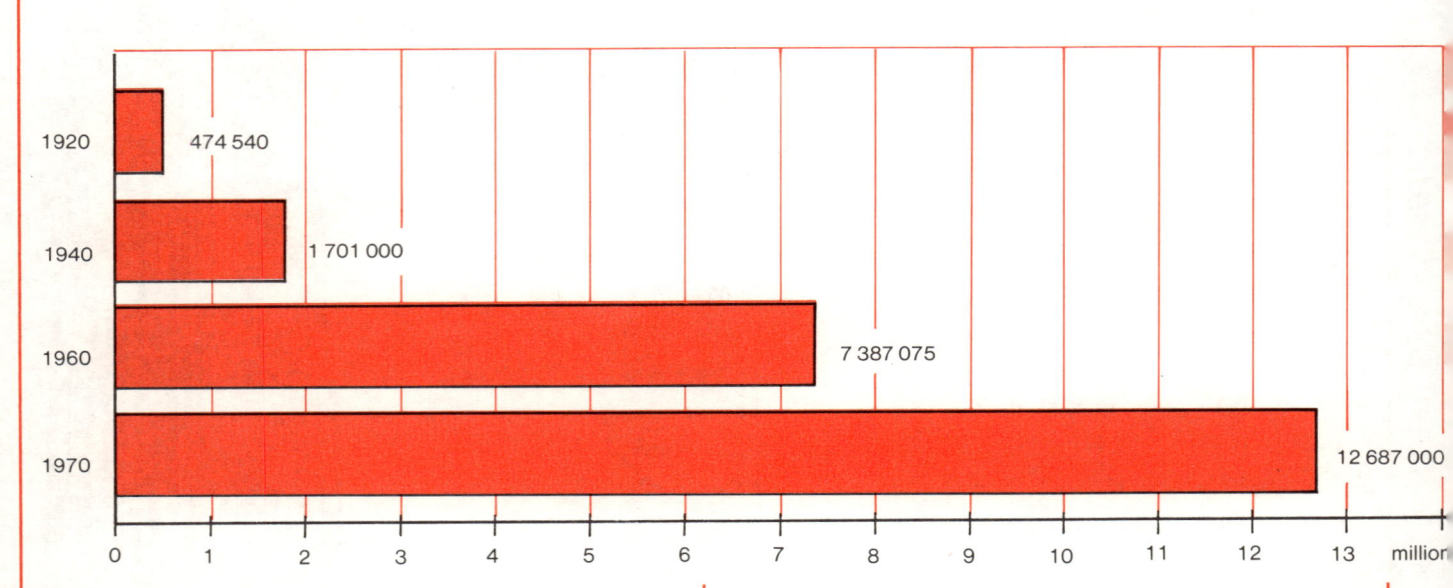

- 1920: 474 540
- 1940: 1 701 000
- 1960: 7 387 075
- 1970: 12 687 000

Table 5.3 Motor car licences issued in UK

Date	Cost
29 May 1922	1½d (½p) approx
1 May 1940	2½d (1p)
15 Feb 1971	3p
20 Aug 1979	10p
5 Apr 1984	16½p

Table 5.4 The cost of a first-class letter in UK

Table 5.4 shows only some of the years when the cost of a first class stamp rose in price. Note that until September 1968 all mail went first class. Second class stamps are slightly cheaper.

1920	10 shillings – (50p)
1946	26 shillings – (£1.30)
1969	£5
1979	£23.30
1984	£34.85

Table 5.5 Old age pensions for single person per week

The figures in Table 5.5 are the amounts of money a pensioner would receive from the government pension every week.

Activities

Now that you have read these tables carefully, and have looked at the pictures, answer the following questions:

1. How many Conservative Prime Ministers have there been since 1924?
2. Which political party was in power in December 1964?
3. How much would a single pensioner receive in 1946?
4. Which political party was in power in 1946? How do you know?
5. When was second class mail introduced?
6. Which figures are **not** included in Table 5.3?
7. According to Table 5.2 how much did a female worker earn in 1940?
8. According to Table 5.2 how much more did a male worker earn at the same time?
9. On what date was the 3p stamp for letters first issued?
10. Who became Prime Minister on 18 Oct 1963?
11. Name the politicians who were Prime Minister more than once between 1925 and 1980.
12. In which year was a single person's pension £23.30?
13. For how long was Neville Chamberlain Prime Minister?
14. How many car licences were issued in 1960?
15. How many more car licences were issued in 1970?

Fig. 5.2 Harold Wilson

More Activities

The following questions are more difficult because you will have to look at more than one table to find the answers.

(a) What was a male manual worker's wage when Ramsay MacDonald was **first** Prime Minister?

(b) How many car licences were issued in the year when a female worker's average wage was £7.40?

(c) In which year was the price of a stamp 2½d, and 1 701 000 car licences issued?

(d) Who was Prime Minister in August of the same year?

(e) How many Prime Ministers were Knights?

(f) How much was the single person's weekly pension when Harold Wilson was in his last year as Prime Minister for the first time?

(g) By how much has the price of a stamp increased from 1971 to 1984?

(h) If you were a male manual worker in 1940 how much would you have left out of your wages if you bought forty postage stamps?

(i) By how much did the wages of female workers rise between the years 1924 and 1978? Which political party was in power in the years 1924 and 1978?

(j) How many days before Winston Churchill became PM for the first time was the 2½d stamp introduced? How much did a female worker earn at the same time?

By answering these questions correctly you should have gathered more information from them than you first thought. Any information like this is useful in any aspect of historical study and these particular figures could be helpful in the project section of Volume 3.

Summary

1. Figures, as well as words, can provide useful facts for the historian.
2. When using **statistics** or charts of this kind always read them very carefully – including the title.
3. Information of this kind can help to give a positive picture of what life was like in past years.

Unit 6

Measurement of time

Most things in our lives are measured in some way. Your height is measured in metres and centimetres, your weight in kilograms and grams, your money in pounds and pence. Time is also measured and so, therefore, is history.

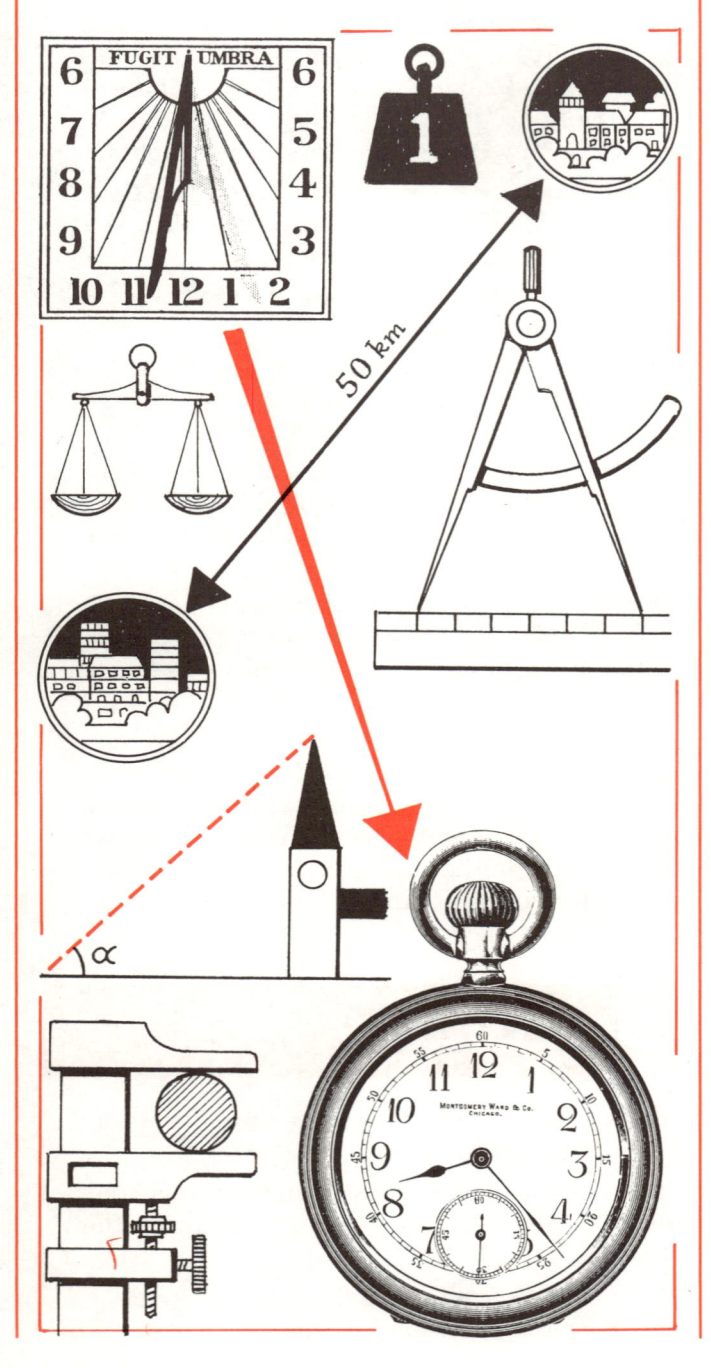

We measure immediate time in seconds. A woman running the 100 metres will be thinking of breaking the tape within seconds, tenths and hundredths of seconds from the start. A man running the 3000 metres will finish it in minutes, seconds, tenths and hundredths of seconds. A man running a Marathon will finish in hours, minutes, seconds, tenths and hundredths of seconds. The longer the race the longer the time, and the greater the divisions of time. It is the same with history, the further back in time we go, the more ways there are of measuring the time or naming periods of it.

6.1 Years

Historical time is not calculated in the same way as the track judges measure a race because historians are not usually interested in what happened tenths of seconds ago. The usual measurement for historical time is in **years**. Certain numbers of years together are given certain names to distinguish them. What name is given to the following examples?

(a) 10 years
(b) 100 years
(c) 1000 years

6.2 Ages

If we study the life of man, the length of time that he has been on the earth is very long, approximately 1.6 million years. Such a figure is extremely difficult to understand. We have no idea how long 1 600 000 years is. To help a little, historians have divided up this vast time into smaller sections. Until recent times each section took the name of the basic material used during that particular period of history. For example, the Stone Age is so called because man's tools and weapons were made from flint and stones; the Bronze Age, because early man had by then discovered the process of making bronze.

6.3 Centuries

In more recent history the historian often refers to the **century** during which an event happened as well as the actual year. For example, you may read, or be told, that the English Civil War took place in the 17th century. But you may say that the Civil War occurred in the 1640s, why are the 1640s in the 17th century? This is very easy to explain.

Most people in Europe start the measurement of time from the year Christ was born, we call this year AD 1. The initials AD stand for the Latin words **Anno Domini** meaning 'In the year of our Lord'. Dates before the birth of Christ are followed by the letters BC which simply mean 'before Christ'.

You will see in Table 6.1 that the years AD 1 to AD 99 are called the 1st century, because it is the first 100 years. The years from AD 100 to AD 199 is the 2nd century, and so on.

So you see that a year beginning 16 hundred and something is in the 17th century and something beginning 19 hundred and something is in the 20th century: the number of the century is always one more than the 'hundred' number of the year.

6.4 Historical periods

Some historians refer to **periods** of history, for example, Saxon times or Norman times. These names are given to cover a number of years or in some cases centuries. They can give the reader an immediate idea as to the time in history being discussed and can be used as an aid to put historical years into some sort of order. If you learn the third column of Table 6.1 you will come to know, for example, that the Saxon time came a long time before the Tudor time, and this will help you put historical facts about these times into **perspective.**

Sometimes historical periods are given the name of the ruling royal family of that time. The 16th century is called the Tudor age because the **Tudor** family was the royal family throughout that century. The names of these periods of history are marked on the chart at the appropriate time.

AD 1 – AD 99	1st century AD	
AD 100 – AD 199	2nd century AD	
AD 200 – AD 299	3rd century AD	
AD 300 – AD 399	4th century AD	
AD 400 – AD 499	5th century AD	
AD 500 – AD 599	6th century AD	
AD 600 – AD 699	7th century AD	Anglo-Saxon
AD 700 – AD 799	8th century AD	
AD 800 – AD 899	9th century AD	
AD 900 – AD 999	10th century AD	* Saxon
AD 1000 – AD 1099	11th century AD	
AD 1100 – AD 1199	12th century AD	Norman
AD 1200 – AD 1299	13th century AD	Angevin
AD 1300 – AD 1399	14th century AD	Plantagenet
AD 1400 – AD 1499	15th century AD	Lancastrian
AD 1500 – AD 1599	16th century AD	Tudor
AD 1600 – AD 1699	17th century AD	Stuart
AD 1700 – AD 1799	18th century AD	Georgian
AD 1800 – AD 1899	19th century AD	Regency (1800–1820) Victorian (1837–1901)
AD 1900 – AD 1999	20th century AD	Edwardian (1900–1914)

Table 6.1 Time chart

6.5 BC and AD

If you look at Fig 6.3 it will help you to understand how long man has stayed in these various stages of development. The scale used is 1 centimetre to 100 000 years. We consider ourselves very modern but as you can see from the diagram the **Modern Age**, dating from AD 1485, takes up only

Unit 6 continued

a very small portion of the complete picture. We show the years after the birth of Christ with the letters AD and the years before Christ with BC. However, all the years are numbered from the year 1; for example:

$$300-200-100-1-100-200-300$$
$$\text{BC} \qquad\qquad\qquad\qquad \text{AD}$$

Therefore, from the year 100 BC to AD 100 there are 200 years: 100 – 1 – 100. If you want to find out the number of years between a year with BC after it and another with AD before it, you simply add the two figures together; for example, a man was born in 48 BC and died in AD 36, he was therefore 84 years old at his death.

The years from 99 BC to 1 is called the 1st century BC, the years 199 BC to 100 BC the 2nd century BC and so on.

Activities

Questions

1 In which centuries are the following years?

(a) AD 1726   (f) AD 824
(b) AD 1864   (g) AD 1641
(c) AD 708   (h) AD 1512
(d) AD 436   (i) AD 999
(e) AD 1926   (j) AD 1326

2 How many years are there between the following dates?
(example: 58 BC – 36 BC Ans = 22 years)

(a) 36 BC – AD 10
(b) 210 BC – AD 100
(c) 96 BC – AD 4
(d) 51 BC – AD 44
(e) 512 BC – AD 336

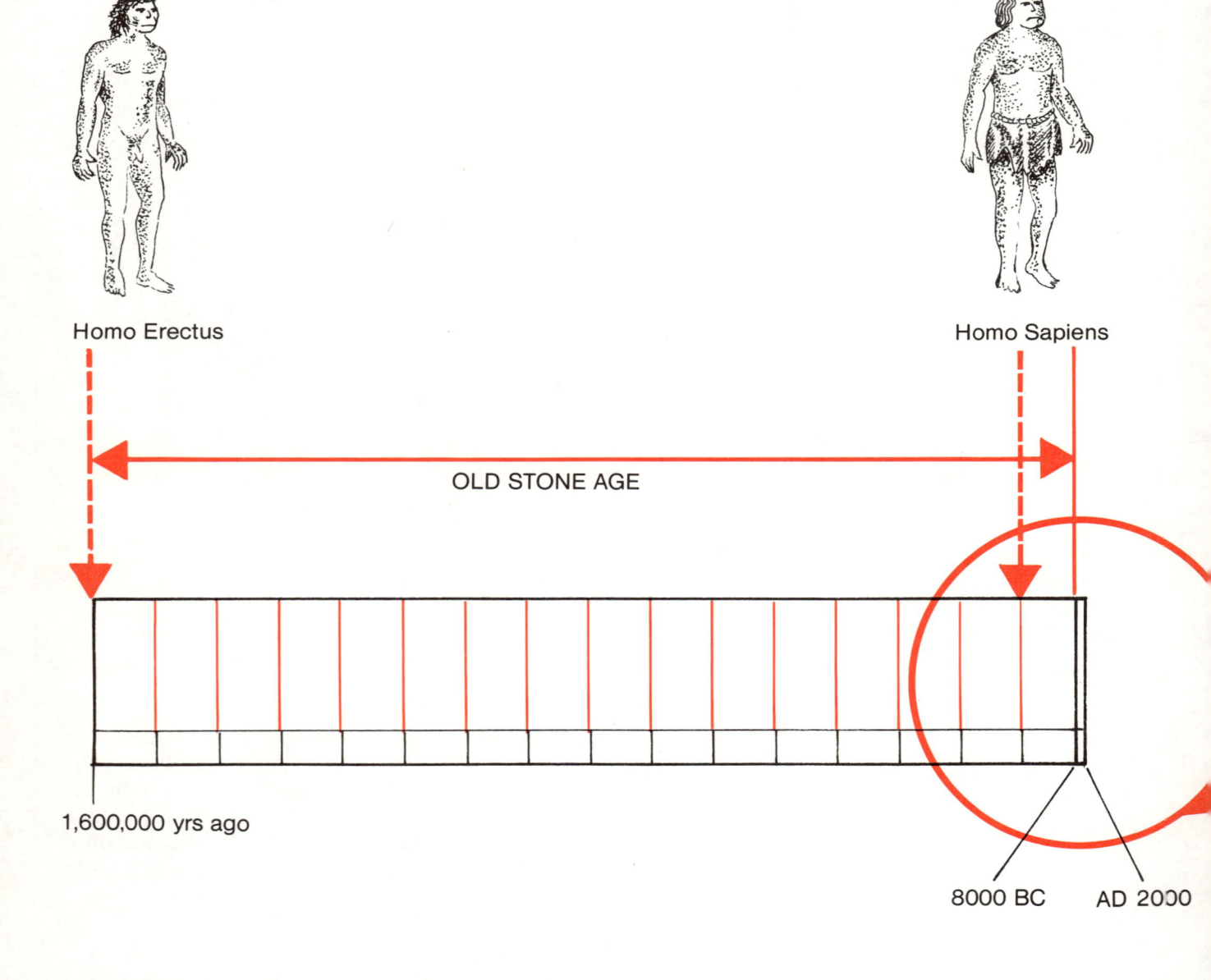

Fig. 6.3 Graph showing the time scale of man

Homo Erectus — OLD STONE AGE — Homo Sapiens

1,600,000 yrs ago

8000 BC   AD 2000

Summary

1. All historical time is measured – usually in years.
2. Different lengths of historical time have different names e.g. 10 years = a decade.
    100 years = one century
    1000 years = one millenium
3. In Britain, centuries are often named after the ruling royal family of the time.
4. A large number of centuries is often referred to as an **Age**. However, an Age can also be used to describe a single century or less e.g. the Elizabethan Age (1558 – 1603).
5. All years, in most European countries, are measured from the year 1.
6. All years before 1 have the letters BC (**before Christ**) after them.
7. All years after 1 have the letters AD (**Anno Domini**) before them.

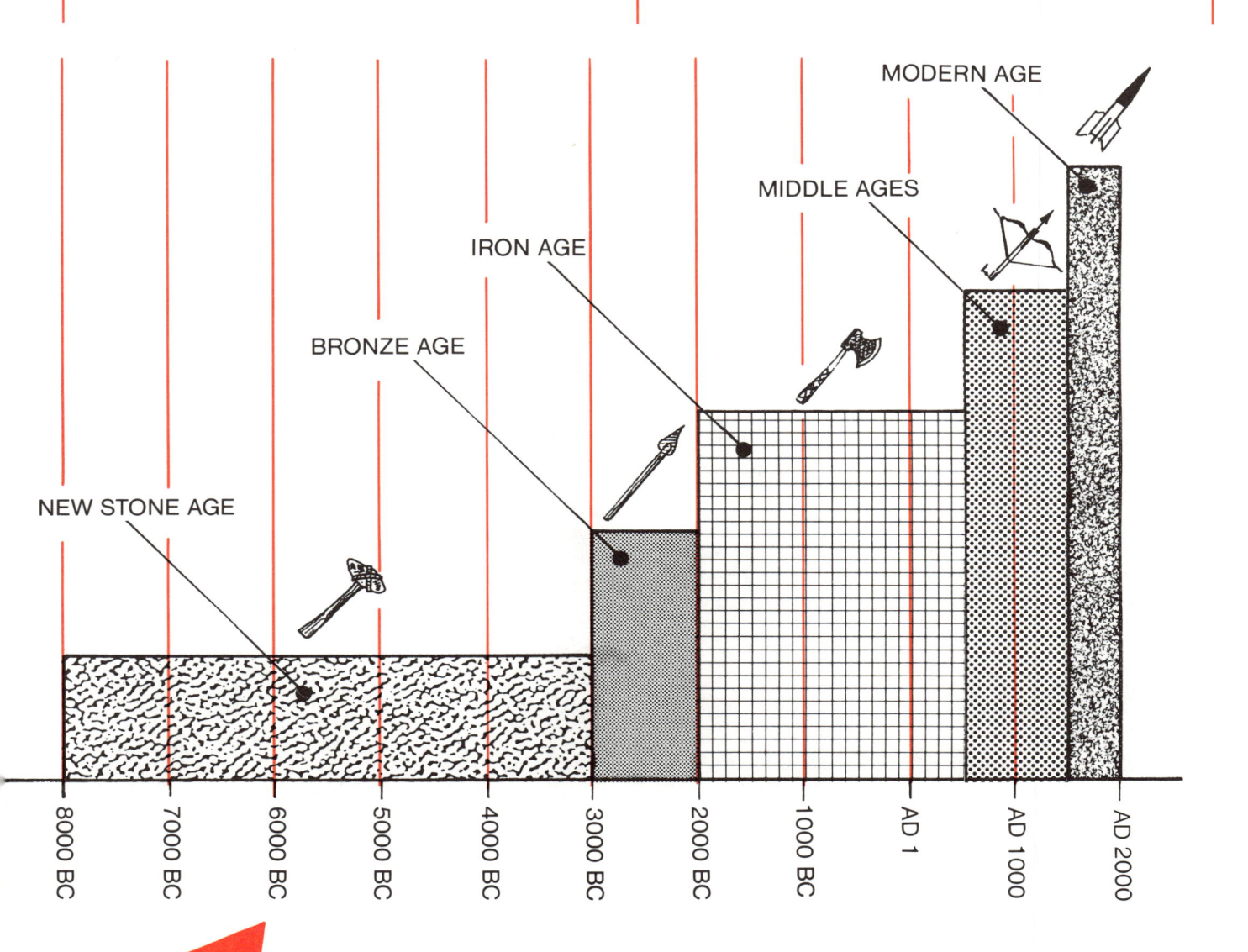

Unit 7

People in pictures

In the previous units we looked at various historical time scales. We started with your own history over a short period of time, then your parents and grandparents spanning a longer period and finally, in the last chapter we labelled the centuries back to 1 AD. But as well as looking at events and time, the historian needs to look at the characters involved during these various periods of history.

If you read a play at school, the first page usually has a list of characters. It gives the names of the people in the play and often a brief description of what he or she is like. History is very similar: the play is made up of historical events that have occurred and the list of characters are the kings, queens, bishops, soldiers and common people who have taken part in these events.

7.1 Clues to identity

But who were these people, what did they look like and what clues can we look for to help us work out when they lived? Look at Fig. 7.1. You will see this person almost every week on television, either taking part in state occasions, or opening new buildings or meeting foreign heads of state. You see her so often that you do not even have to think before you say who she is. But, look at Fig. 7.2. Do you know who this is? If you do not, what in the picture could give us a clue as to when this person lived. There is a very obvious clue. Look at what this person is wearing. Do ladies dress like this now? You could take this picture to your school and compare it with those in books of fashion, or fashion through the ages; most libraries have series of books of this kind. Start your search with the most recent fashions and work backwards until you find an illustration very similar to this one. You will then discover the time in which the character lived and I am sure you could then work out who it is. (The answer is in the Answers section on page 124.)

Fig. 7.1

Fig. 7.2

The two examples we have used are quite simple and there is a great deal written about both characters. If you wanted to find out more about them you would need only to visit your local library, find a book on Queen Elizabeth I or II and take notes on all the information you required. However, not all the members of our historical play have books written about them.

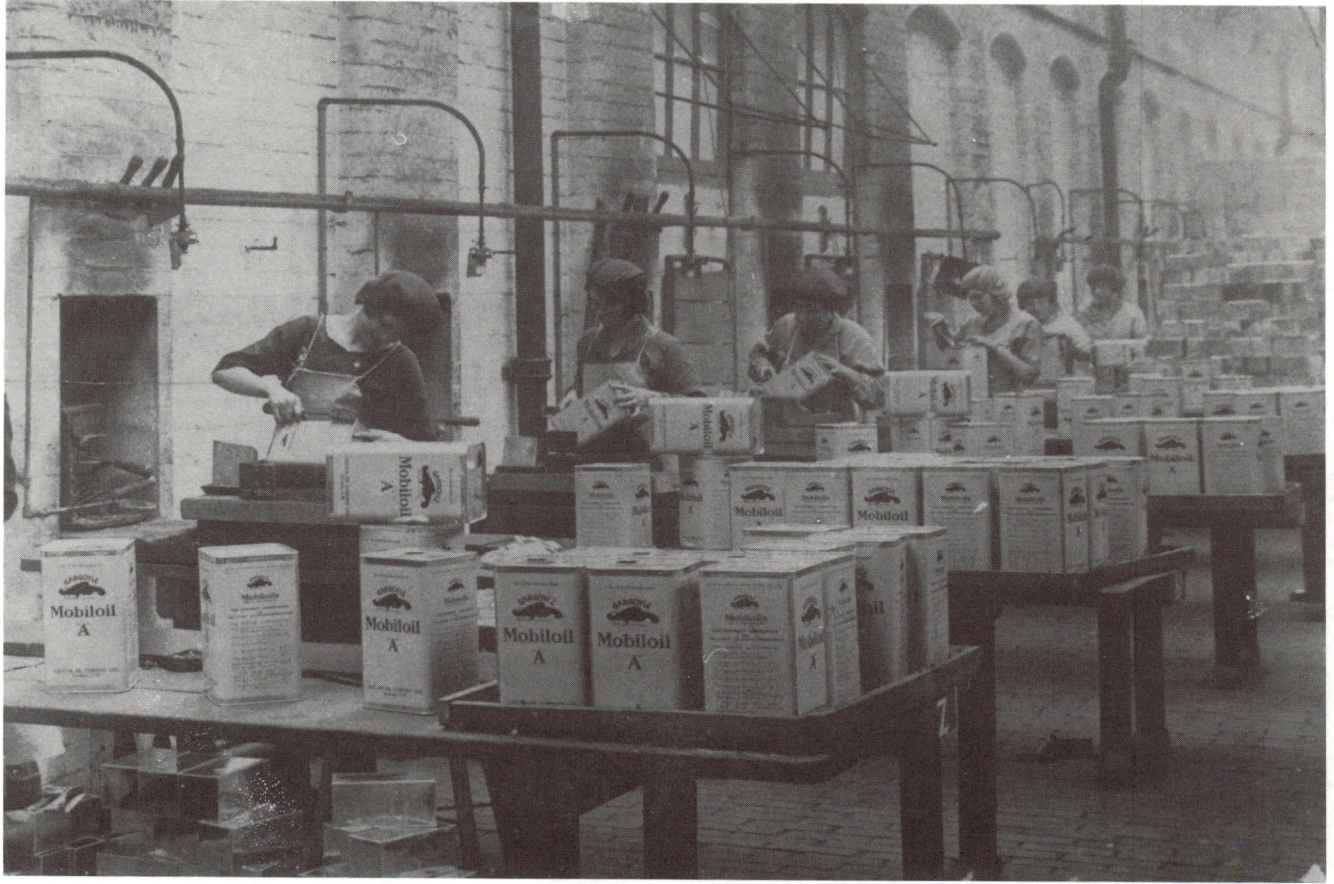

Fig. 7.3

7.2 Extracting information

Look at Fig. 7.3. What do you think is happening here? This photograph is very different from the other two because the people in it are not well known and are not famous. However, we can **extract** a lot of useful information from it. You will see an illustration similar to this in Unit 16 and you will be shown how to find out more from a picture of this kind than you thought possible. This picture could be important to the historian because it shows working conditions in a factory of the 1920s and it could tell him how the work in a factory of this kind was carried out. (Many pictures of this nature will help you in your project in Volume 3.)

One important thing to remember is that Figs. 7.1 and 7.3 are more accurate than Fig. 7.2 because they are actual photographs of the subject concerned. Fig. 7.2 is a painting and it must be remembered that the artist was unlikely to paint a portrait of a king or queen or other important person, which was not to their liking, otherwise, he would soon find himself out of a job. Therefore, although this painting gives us a reasonable likeness of the person concerned, the historian cannot use it as if it were completely accurate. What it does do, however, is to give the reader a very good indication of the clothing and fashion of the time, and the style of portrait painting.

Activities

Questions

1 Look at Fig. 7.1 –

(a) Who is the subject of the picture?
(b) In which year did she come to the throne? (**Not** the year of her coronation.)
(c) The text suggested three reasons why you might see her on the television, what are they?

2 Look at Fig. 7.2 –

(a) Who is the subject of the picture?
(b) During which years was she Queen?
(c) During which **two** centuries did her reign occur?

3 Look at Fig. 7.3 –

(a) What will the tins in the picture eventually contain?
(b) Can you describe what the women have in their right hands.
(c) Make a list of all the similar articles of clothing that you can see being worn by the women.
(d) Why do you think they are wearing the aprons and caps?
(e) When was the photograph taken?

Unit 8

People in written sources

As well as gaining information about historical characters from paintings, drawings and photographs we also need to be able to extract **relevant** facts from a variety of written sources. Below is an example of a description of a famous person whose death is celebrated each year on 5 November – Guy Fawkes.

The apprehension of Guy Fawkes

'He was born Guido Fawkes, a Protestant. He was later converted to the Roman Catholic Church. He served two years with the Spanish army in Flanders. He had been on a mission to King Philip III of Spain to persuade him to invade England.

He joined the Gunpowder Plot, an attempt by a group of English Catholics to blow up the Houses of Parliament together with James I and all his peers. Calling himself John Johnson he became the caretaker of the cellar rented by Thomas Percy for the purpose of storing thirty-six barrels of gunpowder. At 11.00 p.m. on the night of 4 November 1605 Fawkes was seized in the cellar by a group of soldiers under the leadership of a magistrate. He was tied up and taken to the Tower. Fawkes, with the other surviving plotters, was tried on 26 January 1606 and executed on 30 January in the same year.'

Notice that although this is a very simple outline of Guy Fawkes' life, there is a lot more information in this brief passage which would be useful to you if you were studying this particular time in history. You, as an historian, would need to be able pick out the relevant fact or facts that you required to answer a **specific** question.

8.1 Extracting information

You will see what other facts we can find from this passage by answering the questions in the 'Activities' section. Some of the answers will be easy, but some will require more thought.

When reading a passage like this you should always ask yourself a series of questions similar to those you will be asked in 'Activities'. They will help you focus all your attention on the writing. The simplest way to remember the facts is to write them down in a rough book as a series of notes. You could always add to these later and keep them for use at a later date. Remember you need only keep a record of the important facts and you do not need to write down the questions, only ask them to yourself as you read the material. The more you read the extract the more facts you will remember from it, especially if you take notes.

8.2 Newspapers

As well as using written material from history books or journals or diaries, we can see living history in our morning or evening newspapers. Although, as you will see in Units 35 and 36, the historian has to be careful how he uses newspapers as a source of information, they can provide useful background material, and the instant, on-the-spot reporting can provide 'atmosphere' and bring the history to life. Look at the example of an imaginary newspaper report in 1644. As you read it through ask yourself questions about it. There are no set questions to this piece, so test yourself after you have read it and see how much you have remembered.

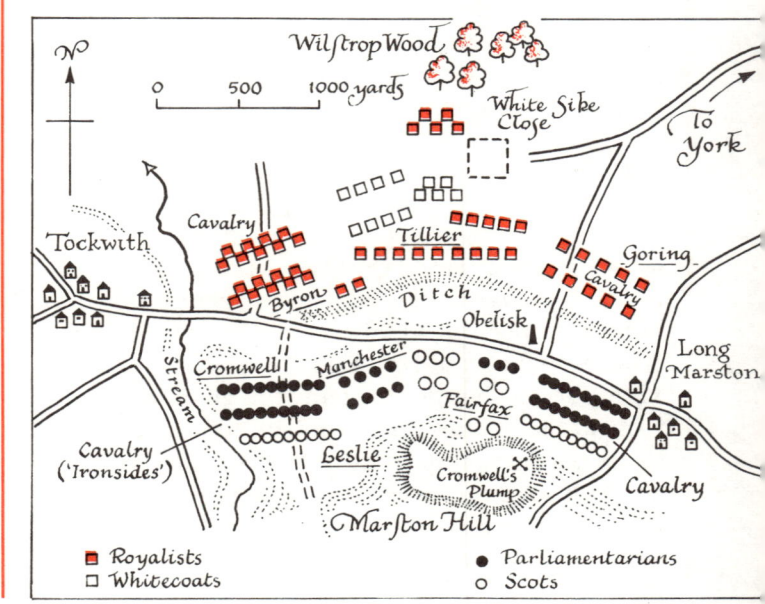

Fig. 8.2 Map showing the battle of Marston Moor

Daily Flag

3rd July 1644

King loses Marston Moor—Northern Army Defeated. Marquis of Newcastle flees to Holland, Prince Rupert hides in bean field.

A.N. Other Civil War Correspondent

'Yesterday after a very confused and noisy battle on the smoky and barren Marston Moor, between Tockwith and Long Marston, the King's army, under the command of his nephew Prince Rupert, was defeated by the superior forces of Cromwell's New Model Army. Although there was a brave, but vain, rearguard action by the Whitecoats of the Marquis of Newcastle, the Royalists were soundly beaten and in consequence the King can no longer put a large mobile army into the field anywhere in the North.

Prince Rupert, having first taken refuge in a bean field, escaped to Chester. The Marquis of Newcastle fled to Holland leaving his soldiers to their plight. The estimated number of dead is approximately 5000. Others fled the field in the confusion, but many wounded still lie where they fell, their screams and groans echoing across the wastes, a grim reminder of the encounter.'

This is how an imaginary correspondent in the English Civil War may have reported from the battle of Marston Moor, (of course no such newspapers existed at the time). The headlines provide a summary of what had taken place and they highlight some of the important events. As we know we cannot consider such a report as completely accurate, but it does supply us with atmosphere and background. The reporter informs us of the main characters and the location of the battle and its outcome. It also tells us what happened after the encounter. All this you would find in a history book covering this period of history, but this account provides us with the feel of the battlefield and tells us exactly what it was like by using words such as: noisy, smoky, barren, groans and screams. It is not necessarily accurate, but informative and alive. The use of newspapers to the historian will be dealt with more fully in Units 35 and 36.

Activities

Questions

(a) What was Guy Fawkes real name?
(b) What religion did he first practise?
(c) Where was the Spanish army fighting when he was a member of it?
(d) Who was the King of Spain at this time?
(e) What religion do you think this King practised? Give reasons for your answer.
(f) What name did Fawkes use as a member of the Gunpowder Plot?
(g) At what time was he arrested?
(h) What is the 'Tower' mentioned in the extract?
(i) How many days were there between his trial and execution?
(j) Which King would have been killed if the plot had been successful?

Further work

1 Using the information provided on Guy Fawkes, and any extra facts you can find out about him, write a newspaper report as if you were a modern crime reporter transported back to the year 1605 witnessing the arrest and trial of Fawkes. Your work will require a headline and you will need to provide atmosphere. However, in this case your information must be historically accurate. You may like to illustrate it.

2 Using one of the examples above i.e. either Guy Fawkes or Marston Moor **summarize** the important **historical** facts provided in the text in no more than four sentences.

Summary

Units 7 and 8

1 People and characters are very important to the history of any country or civilization.

2 We can use photographs, paintings and drawings to help us describe a character.

3 Remember photographs can be more accurate than paintings. The artist had to paint a good picture of his subject. However, paintings can provide us with useful background knowledge.

4 The historian needs to extract information about people and characters from a variety of written sources.

5 Often a written passage can give the historian more facts than a picture and can provide him with a wider description of events at the time.

6 Remember to write down all the important facts when you read any historical extract.

Unit 9

Crafts and trades

People throughout history have always had jobs or trades which in some cases they have continued to follow for most of their lives. These jobs can give us a clue not only to the life of the people themselves, but also to the living conditions of the population in general.

Most jobs today are found in factories, shops or offices of some kind. However, if we go back 300 years to the time of Charles II, a lot of trade was actually carried out in the road. It was not unusual to see a cow being milked on the corner of a London street and the fresh milk being sold on the spot. There was no doorstep delivery. All the street traders had individual cries or catch-phrases to try to persuade passers-by to buy their produce. The only similar example today is the newspaper seller or sometimes a 'rag and bone' man or market trader. Some of these street traders could still be found in some parts of Britain in the early years of this century. At the end of the last century it was very common in London to hear flower-girls singing 'Sweet Lavender' or fruit sellers 'Cherry Ripe' in the hope of selling their wares. (Why do you think people would wish to buy lavender?)

9.1 Making deductions

There are many examples, both written and pictorial (in pictures) of these types of trades, but how do they help the historian? Look at the following list. It contains a number of jobs which may have been seen in London by the diarist Samuel Pepys in 1660:

A milk-carrier, water-carrier, coalman, tinker, rat-catcher, basket-weaver, old-clothes man, chair mender, mouse-trap sellers and bakers.

How many of these jobs can still be found today? You would certainly see a coalman except now he would be delivering it by lorry instead of carrying it on his back. But had you realized that the fact a coalman appears in this list tells us that coal was used as a fuel in London in the 1660s. It is **evident** that a man could make a living as a water-carrier. This can give us a clue to life at the time. (What is it?) Quite simply that the population did not have running water in their houses and they were, in some cases, prepared to pay somebody to bring it from the nearest pump; the same with the milk-carrier.

There were many rat-catchers and people selling mouse-traps, so we know that they had a problem with vermin. Baskets were very popular. How do we know?

9.2 Using a combination of sources

We can use these lists and descriptions to give us a clue to the life of the time, but they tell us little of the conditions of the people working in these trades. For this we often have to use more than one **source** in order to find out our information. Look at the following examples:

1. Life for labourers

In the past, one of the most important staple foods for the working population was bread, for which wheat was needed. Unfortunately the price of wheat rose and fell (fluctuated) for many different reasons. If we look at the average wages for a labourer and at the price of wheat at the same time, it can give a good indication of what life was like for these people.

	1597	1682
Average weekly wage for skilled labourer	2/– (10p)	8/– (40p)
Average weekly wage for unskilled labourer	1/6 (7½p)	4/6 (22½p)
Price of a 2lb (1kg) bag of wheat	4/6 (22½p)	3/– (15p)

You should be able to see immediately that the labourers in 1597 could not afford to buy flour and, therefore, we can assume that either they found something else to eat instead of wheat, or they went hungry. In 1682 the skilled labourer was better off and could afford the wheat, but the unskilled labourer would have had to think very carefully before spending a lot of his wages on this one item.

2. Life for children

You will certainly stay at school until you are 16, but if you had been born into a poor family in the 1840s and 50s your life would have been very different. Firstly, you would not have attended school and if you had lived in a coalmining area you may have been like the children in the example. It is a simplified extract from a government report on the working conditions of children in 1842. (Children's Employment Commission. Report on the Mines.)

> 'The practice of employing children aged only six or seven is very common. The children go down the pit with the men at 4.00 a.m. and remain in the pit for between eleven and twelve hours each day. The child's work is to open and shut the doors of the galleries when the coal trucks pass. For this job a child is trained to sit by itself in a dark passage for the twelve hours he or she is at the mine.'

This extract tells us a great deal about the life of these children. Imagine what it must have been like for them sitting in a damp, dark mine shaft for up to twelve hours, just opening doors. Thankfully things have changed but the quotation refers to something happening only 140 years ago; in historical terms that is a very short time.

9.3 Making further deductions

If you, as an historian, read this report in full, you would get a clear picture of what life was like for these children, not only in the mines, but also outside. For instance, if in winter children went to the mine at 4.00 a.m. and returned at 4.00 p.m. they would spend the whole day in darkness. How do you think this would effect their health? Sunlight provides us with vitamin D; a lack of sun and, therefore, a lack of this vitamin can lead to a disease called Rickets where the bones become bent and **malformed.** This was quite common in the 18th and 19th centuries.

There are many examples like those above and you will come across them in your history lessons or your reading. But remember, as you study them do not take the facts at face value, think about the clues they can give to how the population lived at the time.

Activities

1 Use the figures from example on page 30 and draw a bar chart as follows:

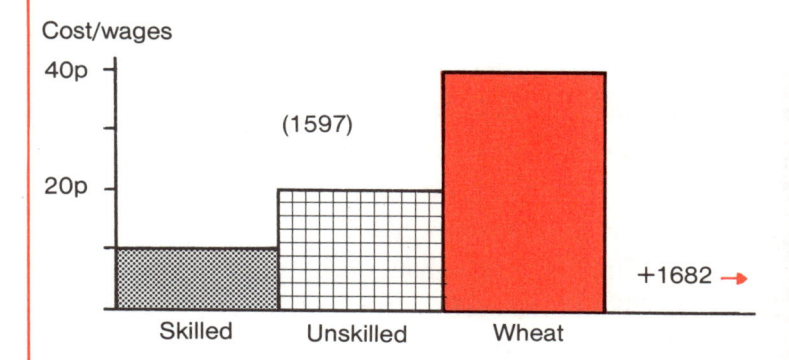

explain, using the text, what these graphs show.

2 Find out about other jobs in the 1800s which were done only by children.

3 Charles Kingsley wrote a famous book about chimney sweeps in Victorian times. Do you know what it is called?

Summary

1 We can look at photographs, drawings and written descriptions of working people. On the face of it they describe only the type of work these people were doing at that time in history, but they can also inform us about the social conditions i.e. what life was like for both the rich and poor.

2 The jobs themselves can provide us with clues to the past: why did they need rat-catchers and water-carriers?

3 By looking at more than one source of information it is possible to answer a simple question about life at the time. For example, by comparing wages with the price of wheat, we can work out if labourers were able to afford the staple foods, and we can link working conditions to health.

Revision Units 1–9

Word search

The answers to the following questions can be found in Units 1–9. Ring them on the chart.

1. Royal family name given to 14th century.
2. Royal family name given to 15th century.
3. Guy Fawkes served in the army of this country.
4. Name given to 9th and 10th centuries.
5. The battle at which King Charles I lost his Northern Army (2 words).
6. The 16th-century royal family.
7. Name given to 13th century.
8. The first twenty years of the 19th century.
9. Name of the years 1837–1901.
10. Fawkes served with an army in this country.
11. King Charles' opponents in the Civil War.
12. Name given to the 12th century.
13. King Charles I's family name.
14. Name given to the 18th century.
15. Fawkes' first name.
16. The name given to a period of ten years.
17. Prince who was Charles I's nephew.
18. Well-known character who wrote a diary in the 1600s (2 words).
19. Travelling odd-job man in 17th and 18th centuries.
20. The name given to a war between people in the same country.
21. . . . Saxons?
22. The title given to male monarch.
23. The name given to a period of 100 years.
24. The name given to a period of 1000 years.
25. The name given to large time periods in history.
26. Your best source of information about your own history.
27. History starts when?
28. What the historian requires when searching for material.
29. Surname of British Prime Minister in 1974.
30. Surname of Liberal Party leader at same time.
31. The material used by early man after stone.
32. Before Christ can be shortened to . . .
33. . . . Domini?
34. Fawkes' original Christian name.
35. Sir Alex Douglas—? PM Oct 1963.

```
E W F L A N D E R S O D E K S
T I A A N P E D I A S P A I N
P L A N T A G E N E T E G N I
A S H C N R F C G D U P E G X
R O S A X O N A V Y A Y S M B
L N A S B C O D M A R S T O N
I J M T P A R E N T T U D O R
A Q U R D E M B R O N Z E T U
M F E I G H A N G L O I J H F
E K L A L A N G E V I N M O E
N C E N T U R Y O N O A G R R
T I N K E R O P R W R Q U P T
H V S T B U R E G E N C Y E V
O I V I C T O R I A N W E N D
M L G U I D O P A T I E N C E
E X M I L L E N N I U M A Z R
```

Unit 10

Detection: a local area

A detective needs to search for, and identify clues. He needs to be able to put the evidence he collects into a correct order or **sequence** and use it to help him solve a mystery or bring someone to trial. The historian also needs to be a detective. He needs to be observant and look closely at his surroundings for certain things which may provide him with clues which either answer, or in some cases raise, certain questions. Some of these clues are obvious and easy to find, some require more searching and some you may look at every day without 'seeing' them. You can be so used to looking at a particular statue or monument that you never think about taking a closer look and finding out its **significance.**

10.1 Keeping your eyes open

A good historical exercise is to go for a walk in your local area, or your nearest town or village, and just look around you. Take a camera with you, if you have one, and photograph or sketch anything you consider to be historical. Remember you are looking out for dates, plaques, statues, and anything else which will provide historical information.

Look closely at Fig. 10.1 and then continue to read the text. It will give you an idea how much simple information can be gained by just keeping your eyes open:

Fig. 10.1 shows a sign outside an inn on the south coast of England. In only a few lines it can give a passer-by information, not only about the inn itself, but also about practices in the local area. For instance, we learn that it was a staging post for the Royal Mail coaches travelling to Wareham. We are told that it was the site of the local market which took place every Friday and that no money changed hands because all the business was conducted by **barter** or as we would call it today **swapping**. The inn was also visited on occasions by the **pressgang**, a group of men who 'kidnapped' others to serve in the Royal Navy's ships, in this case in nearby Poole

Fig. 10.1 This inn sign gives much information to the historian

Unit 10 continued

harbour. We can gather, however, that their task could not have been an easy one because we are told that the local men took refuge in the inn and barricaded the doors. All this information is very simple and **superficial**, but it can always be a starting point for further study. In this case you may wish to learn more about the markets or the pressgang or you may wish to find out the route that the Royal Mail coaches took after they left Wareham.

Fig. 10.2 A battle commemoration stone

10.2 Extracting information

Look at Figs. 10.2 and 10.3. Information is clearly provided in the two examples. Use the following questions to extract it from the pictures.

(a) Who was defeated by King Alfred's Navy on this site?
(b) In which year did the battle take place?
(c) Where did the battle occur?
(d) Who lived in the house in Fig. 10.3?
(e) Whose expedition did he join?
(f) Where did they go?
(g) What was Edgar Evans' nickname?

IN COMMEMORATION
OF A
GREAT NAVAL BATTLE
FOUGHT WITH THE DANES
IN SWANAGE BAY
BY ALFRED THE GREAT
A.D. 877

Fig. 10.3

P.O. EDGAR "TAFFY" EVANS R.N. LEFT HERE IN 1910
TO JOIN CAPTAIN ROBERT FALCON SCOTT ON HIS ILL-FATED
ANTARCTIC EXPEDITION. "TAFFY" EVANS WAS ONE OF
THE FIVE WHO MADE THE FINAL ASSAULT ON THE POLE,
WHICH WAS REACHED ON 18th JANUARY, 1912. ALL FIVE
MEN DIED ON THE 800 MILE RETURN JOURNEY ACROSS THE ICE.

"TO STRIVE, TO SEEK, TO FIND AND NOT TO YIELD"

(h) What date did they reach the South Pole?
(i) What became of the five men who reached the Pole?
(j) How many miles did they have to travel on the return journey?

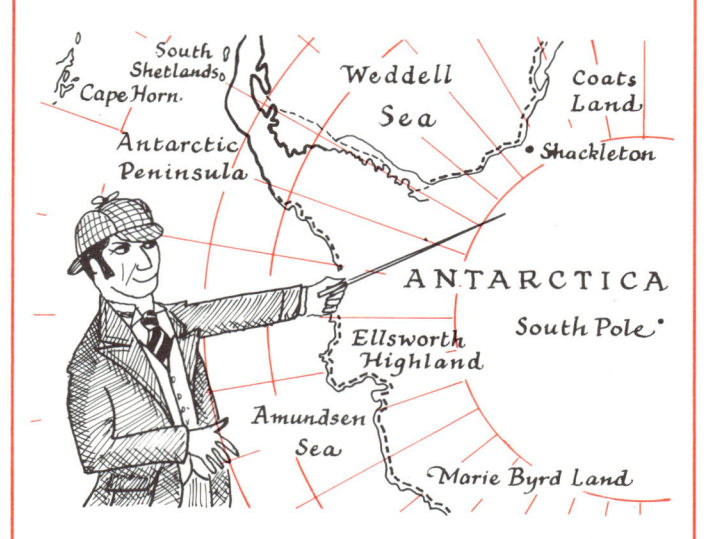

Fig. 10.4 is not so easy. These signs are not very common now except on old houses. It is an **insurance mark**. If a person wanted to insure his house against fire in the 18th century, he would pay the money, or premium, to an insurance company and he would then be given a plaque to put on the outside wall. If the house caught fire at any time the fire-pump, belonging to the insurance company of which he was a member, would put the fire out. If, however, a fire-pump from a rival company came past they would not help because their particular sign was not on the wall. The sign in the photograph is the symbol of the Unity Insurance Company and the number underneath is the insurance number. An historian wishing to date this house would only need to find out when the Unity Company was in existence to have some idea of its age.

10.3 Dates

All the dates in these examples are in English, but many buildings and monuments have their dates in **Latin**. Latin numbers are easy to work out, they just require a little more thought. Below is a list of important Latin numbers to help you.

I = 1, II = 2, III = 3, IV = 4, V = 5, VI = 6,
VII = 7, VIII = 8, IX = 9, X = 10, XX = 20,
XXX = 30, XL = 40 (10 less than 50), L = 50,
LX = 60 (10 more than 50) C = 100, D = 500,
M = 1000.

Fig. 10.4

Activities

Put the following Latin numbers into English
1 XII
2 XXXIII
3 CCLVI
4 MDCCCXXIV
5 DCXXIX

Put these English numbers into Latin
6 42
7 265
8 1850
9 644
10 111

Summary

1 The historian needs the skills of the detective.
2 The historian needs to be observant.
3 Simple information gathered from the surroundings can be a good starting point for further study.
4 Many dates on buildings and monuments are in Latin.

Unit 11

Detection: connections

In Unit 10 you were shown how easy it was to collect simple information by searching your local area. An historian is often unable to answer a question or support a theory by using only one source, so he must be able to see the connection or the relationship between more than one source of information. For example, if you were given a picture of an English king and a plate of burnt cakes and were asked who the king was, your answer would probably be King Alfred because of course it was Alfred who was supposed to have burnt the cakes. You used the simple evidence of the cakes to lead you to your answer by finding the common link between the two pictures.

Activities

In this unit you will be given some very simple sources of information which **may** be connected in one way or another. What you have to do is find the common link, if there is one. Beware, two of the items have nothing to do with the other three.

Read and examine the following examples carefully.

Example A
'The Battle of Edgehill took place in October 1642 in Warwickshire. The Royalist Cavalry, led by King Charles' nephew Prince Rupert, attacked the Parliamentary army and their cavalry was scattered. However, the Prince charged too far away from the battlefield and by the time he returned the Royalist infantry was being attacked by both the Parliamentary infantry and their regrouped cavalry. Sir Edmund Verney, the King's old and trusted standard-bearer, was killed and the King's Royal Standard, a prize possession, was captured and taken back to the Parliamentary lines.'

Fig. 11.1 Sir Edmund Verney

Example B

'The picture shows an example of fashionable ladies' costume of the 1770s. The bodice has a low, wide neck-line with flat trimmings lying over the shoulder. These trimmings also cross at the back and come down either side of the dress to finish at the waist. The sleeves of this type of dress reach only to the elbow where they are joined by long gloves worn over the hands and forearms. The sleeves of an undergarment, a chemise, can be seen beneath the dress sleeves. A lady's hair at this time was brushed back from the forehead, and ringlets at the back were tied up with a small ribbon.'

Example C
'King Charles I was born in 1600. He became King after the death of his father James I. He needed to raise money to pay for his wars against the French and Spanish. He introduced old taxes in order to raise the money. Parliament did not like this and tried to force Charles to stop them. Charles told them they could not object because he was King; he dismissed Parliament in 1629, sent the MPs home and governed the country on his own. Parliament was not recalled until 1640. (This eleven years was called the 'Eleven Years Tyranny'.) When it was eventually recalled, Parliament again refused to allow him to raise money as he wished, so he dissolved it again. It was recalled later. In 1642 Charles tried to arrest five MPs who opposed him, in the House of Commons, but they had fled. Relations between the King and Parliament became worse. Charles left London and went to Nottingham. Later, in October 1642 he came south with his army and fought against Parliament's army at Edgehill, the first battle in the Civil War.'

Fig. 11.2 King Charles I

Example D

'HERE LIETH THE BODY OF THE VALIANT AND MOST WORTHY GENT. SR JOHN SMITH KT. 3D SON OF SR. FRANC:SMITH OF WOOTEN-WAWEN IN YE COUNTY OF WARWICK. BT (DESCENT OF YE ANCIENT FAMILY OF CARINGTON, FROM SR MICHAEL CARINGTON, STANDARD BEARER TO K: RICHARD YE 1ST IN YE HOLYLAND) WHO WITH HIS OWNE HANDS, REDEEMED IN YE BATTEIL OF EDGEHILL YE BANNER ROYAIL OF HIS MOST SACRED MAJESTIE CHARLES 1ST FOR WHICH SIGNAIL VALOUR HE YEN RECEIVED IN YE FIELD Y HONOUR OF KNIGHTHOOD FRO HIS MAJESTIE. SINCE WCH TIME HE IN SEVERAIL BATTEILS GAVE SINGULAR TESTIMONIE OF HIS LOYALTIE AND COURAGE ESPECIALLY IN YE MEMORABLE FIGHT AT BRAMDEAN IN HAMPS. YE 29 OF MARCH WHERE HAVEING REC: SEVERAL WOUNDS IN PSUIT OF VICTORY DIED AT ANDOVER YE 30TH MAR: 1644 WAS YE 1ST OF APRIL HERE INTERD WITH GREAT SOLEMNITY. AGED 28.

Sir Frances Throckmorton of Great Cought in ye County of Warwick BT: (His sister's son) at his charg this Marble hath laid.'

(Taken from a tomb in the Military Chapel, Christchurch, Oxford.)

Unit 11 continued

Example E

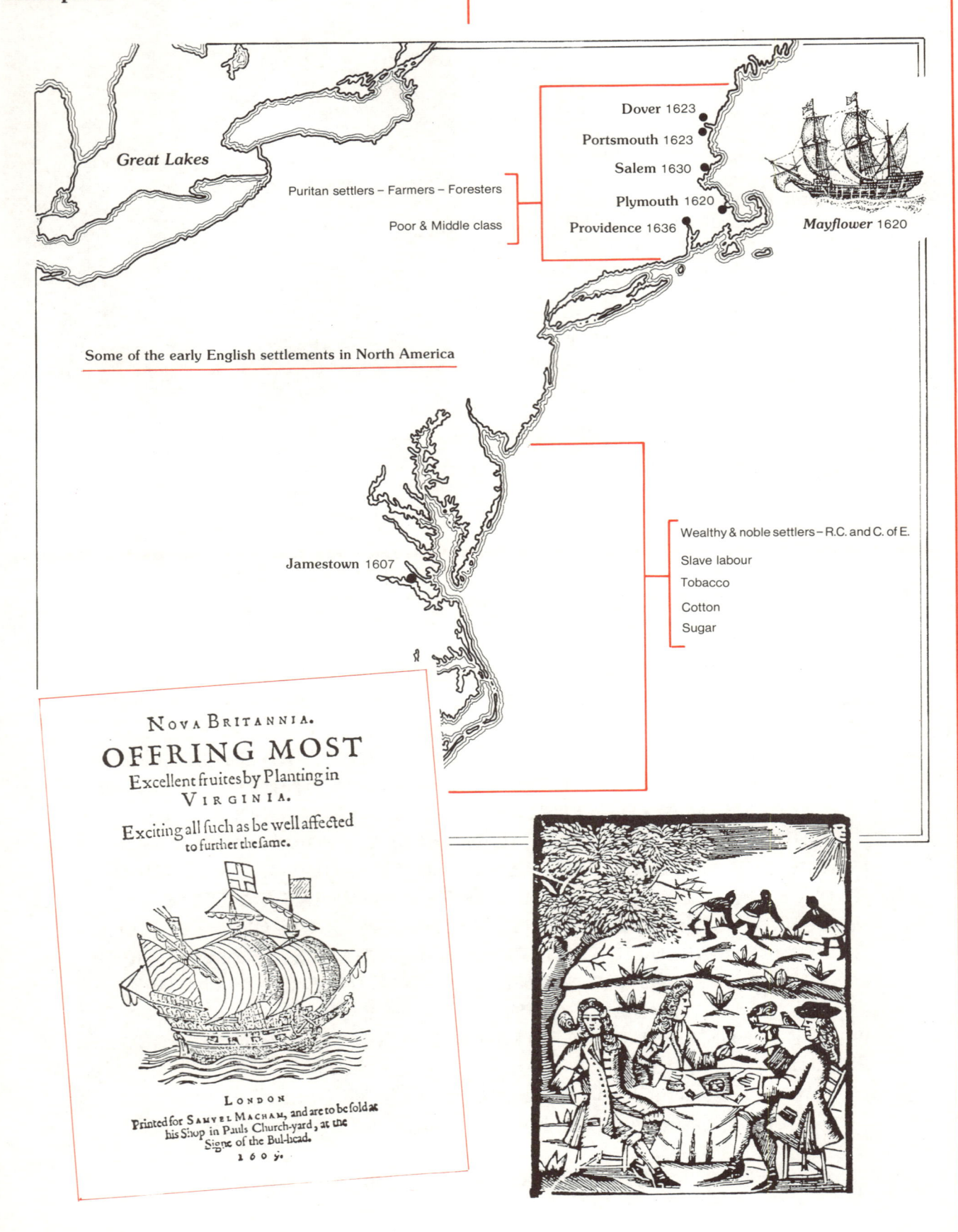

Some of the early English settlements in North America

Dover 1623
Portsmouth 1623
Salem 1630
Plymouth 1620
Providence 1636

Puritan settlers – Farmers – Foresters
Poor & Middle class

Mayflower 1620

Great Lakes

Jamestown 1607

Wealthy & noble settlers – R.C. and C. of E.
Slave labour
Tobacco
Cotton
Sugar

NOVA BRITANNIA.
OFFRING MOST
Excellent fruites by Planting in
VIRGINIA.
Exciting all such as be well affected
to further the same.

LONDON
Printed for SAMVEL MACHAM, and are to be sold at
his Shop in Pauls Church-yard, at the
Signe of the Bul-head.
1609.

Questions

You have now read and closely examined the five examples. Remember there is a very strong link between three of them. Before you find the connection, what information can you extract from the sources? As you answer the following questions try to think of any common link between them. There are many clues!

1. In which year did the Battle of Edgehill take place?
2. Who was the King at the time of the English Civil War?
3. Who was the nephew of the King who was in command of the Royalist Cavalry?
4. What happened to the King's Royal Standard during the battle?
5. Who was the King's standard-bearer?
6. Who was the father of Charles I?
7. Was Britain at war when Charles first came to the throne? Against whom?
8. What name is given to the time that Charles ruled without Parliament?
9. What did Charles try to do in the House of Commons in 1642 which angered the MPs?
10. Where did Charles go when he left London?
11. Where was the first battle of the Civil War?
12. Is there any connection between Examples A and C? If so what is it?
13. In Example D, who is buried in the tomb?
14. Which part of England did he come from?
15. What did this man do at the Battle of Edgehill which made the King knight him?
16. In which battle was he wounded?
17. Where, and when did he die?
18. How old was he when he died?
19. What relation was Sir Frances Throckmorton to the man in the tomb?
20. Is there any connection between Examples A and D? If so what is it?
21. Is there any connection between Examples C and D? If so what is it?
22. When was the dress in Example B fashionable?
23. What was the garment called which was worn under the dress?
24. Describe the fashion in hairstyles at this time in history?
25. Is there any connection between Examples B and A, or C or D? If so what is it?
26. On the map in Example E, two places were established in 1623, what were they?
27. Where did the *Mayflower* land in 1620?
28. Which type of people settled in the Southern parts of North America?
29. Is there any connection between Example E and the others? If so what is it?

Having looked at all the sources and answered all the questions you should be able to see the connection or link between them. One of the sources is very definitely the odd one out, another is loosely linked, but three are very closely related. If you still cannot see the common fact between the extracts, read them all again, find the link and then check your answer at the back of the book.

In Unit 12 we will take this skill one step further and see how we can use more than one source of information and more difficult material to answer a specific question.

Unit 12

Detection: a combination of sources

In Unit 10 we saw how it was possible to find out simple facts from a local area. We looked at four different sources and extracted the details we required. All the information was easily found. Occasionally an historian will come across a piece of evidence which 'makes him curious', and causes him to ask certain questions to help him find out more about it.

In this unit we will imagine you are the historian who has found this unusual evidence. You will be given three photographs taken in and around the town of Swanage in Dorset. The piece of information which has caused you to ask further questions is Fig. 12.1, the London street bollard. The question you have asked yourself is 'What is a London street bollard doing in the middle of Swanage?'

Having asked yourself this question you then, in your seaching, find two further pieces of evidence, Figs. 12.2 and 12.3. At first the three pictures may not seem to be connected, but in fact they are. What you have to do is find out how. Below are three descriptions of the photographs. They contain simple facts you would easily find if you visited the library or museum in Swanage and searched through the useful books on local history. Read these descriptions carefully, and using the information provided in them, answer the question you have already asked yourself.

Description Fig. 12.1
This is a photograph of an old London street bollard. These were put up on the corners of streets to stop large waggons damaging the buildings, pavements and pedestrians as they went by. Originally they were made from broken military cannons which were of no use to the army. These were turned upside down, had a cannon ball wedged into the mouth and erected on street corners. This example has the letters CH^{T}MIDDX CH 1819 stamped on it. This not only

Fig. 12.1

gives the date of origin, 1819, but also the area it came from in Middlesex, because CH^{T}CH stands for Christchurch. When the streets in many areas of London were repaired, a lot of the bollards were no longer required. Many of these bollards came to Swanage by boat.

Description Fig. 12.2
This is a modern photograph of a quarryman splitting a large piece of Purbeck stone in a quarry near Swanage. There is a great deal of this type of stone lying just beneath the surface of the fields in this area, so there are many modern quarries. The stone, however, has been used since as far back as Roman times, and in the 13th

Fig. 12.2

century, it was used in the building of many cathedrals in England including Lincoln, Exeter and Durham. Later in the 18th and 19th centuries it was used to 'face' important buildings in London and also to construct pavements. One of the important builders in London at this time was George Burt of Swanage. The stone was taken by horse and cart to the quay at Swanage where it was put into boats and taken to London.

Description Fig. 12.3
This photograph shows part of a narrow-gauge trackway on the quay at Swanage. It was originally intended to go from the local quarries to the quay, a distance of approximately 6 miles, to make it easier to transport stone to the boats.

Fig. 12.3

However, the system was never completed and the coming of a national railway link in 1885 meant that the trackway would no longer be required because the stone could now go to London and beyond by train.

Finding the link
Are you any nearer answering your question? Have you found any clues which will help you? Before reading on go through these descriptions again and write down anything you think they have in common. Remember you are looking for a link between the three.

Now read the following and you should see the answer.

In this area of the South coast there has always been an important stone-quarrying industry. The description of Fig. 12.2 informs the reader that this stone was used for the building of many cathedrals in England and many of the buildings in London. Before the coming of the railway in 1885 this stone was transported to London by boat (description of Fig. 12.3). However, once these boats had reached their destination and unloaded their cargo they then had to return to Swanage empty. The owners therefore needed to find 'ballast' to help them balance their ships on the return journey. They used anything they could find that was heavy (for a big clue read the last line of the description of Fig. 12.1). Does this answer your question? After some of the new kerbstones and pavements had been laid in London, many of the street bollards were taken up by the builders and stored in their yards. One of these builders, as the description of Fig. 12.2 tells us, was George Burt of Swanage, so it was easy for him to use these bollards as ballast on his boats. When they arrived in Swanage they were used for various things, gate-posts, etc, so that is why the photograph of the street bollard was taken in Swanage and not in London. Could you see the link between the photographs? They all had something to do with the stone-quarrying industry either as ballast, working the stone, or transporting it.

By looking at the three examples together and reading the descriptions carefully you should have been able to answer some part of your original question, but if you only worked out that they all had something to do with stone-working you were halfway there and did well.

Summary

Units 11 and 12

1 Historians often need to ask themselves questions about evidence or information in order to concentrate their area of study.

2 An historian needs to be able to look at more than one source of information and extract the **relevant** clues to answer a specific question.

3 You will find in the course of your study that much of what you read in your searching for an answer to a question is not required. An historian has to decide what information is useful and what is not. He needs to **discriminate** (this will be dealt with more fully in Unit 13).

Revision Units 1–12

Treasure trail

On some occasions the historian has more than enough information to answer a question, but before he can do so, he needs to put that information into some sort of order. Below you will find a similar problem. You have plenty of facts available to enable you to reach the treasure chest, but because the diary containing the details has broken in your hands, the pages are no longer in the correct order. However, if you read each entry carefully you will find many clues which will help you put them into their correct place, and so lead you to the treasure.

1 Left Newlyn harbour Sun 28 Nov in the year of our Lord 1667. Wind WSW. Sea calm. Weather clear. Sailed towards Scillies. Took on water at St Marys. Stayed for two days.

2 Found Turks Island 21°31′N 70°30′W in the West Indies. Took in sail and anchored in the lee of the island in the eighth year of the reign of our good King Charles. Despatched long-boat with seven crew, the mate and myself. Time 1300 hrs.

3 Made framework to take weight of chest. Weak, slight fever. Mate died during the night.

4 Very weak, last entry. May God have mercy. 2 March 1668.

5 Continued west. Caught in storm of the Azores. Took refuge at Porto Delgado, in San Miguel. Rode out storm for three days.

6 Found Twin Peaks. Flies a problem. Took bearing. Located area of dig. Pitched camp near Black Cave.

7 Turks Island, head inland from Pacace Bay. Steady walk for two days. Find Twin Peaks bearing 21°33′N 71°55′W. Chest buried 2 feet beneath surface. Follow the instructions in this log.

8 Winds light to moderate ten days without sight of land.

9 21.30 Large chest lifted from hole. Wooden metal-braced. Locked in four places. As yet impossible to open. Problem of flies worse.

10 Simpson died this morning. We are not going to make it. Have reburied treasure just beneath the surface. Instructions for finding it as below.

11 Two men return with boat, remainder with equipment, venture inland.

12 Remained in camp a further four days. Three of us left. Will attempt the return to the coast tomorrow.

13 27 Jan 11.15 Soil easy, but heat intense. Two of the men very weak. 1600 hrs excitement in digging party. Spades strike metal object.

14 Start a dig early. Twelve spaces NNW of the cave 25 Jan in the year of our Lord 1668.

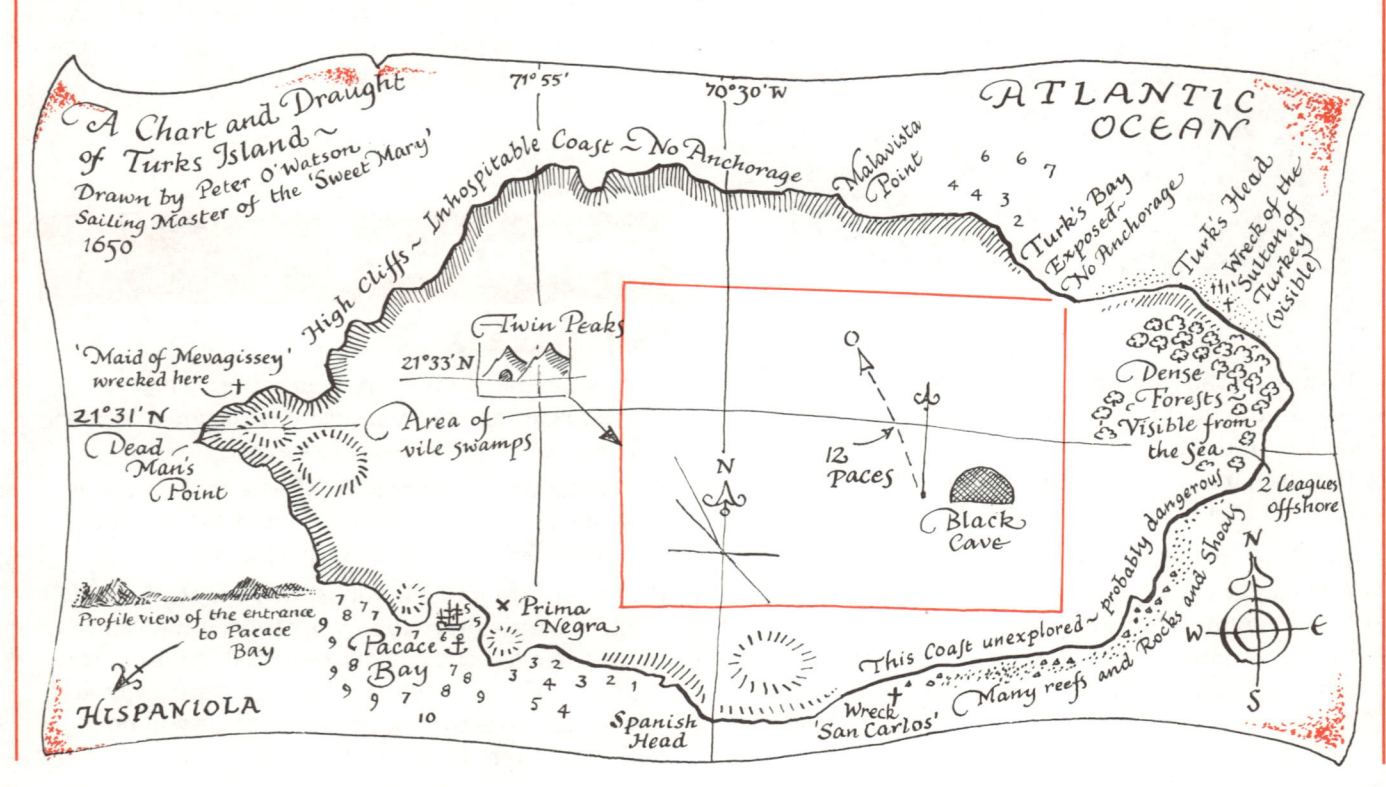

Unit 13

Problem of evidence

Usually the historian needing to answer a specific question has not enough information available to solve it. If this is the case he has to search further afield in order to find the relevant material. By this means he is searching only for certain clues; he is choosing between those which he will find useful and those which he will not.

Although it can be a problem solving a query with too little information, it can be just as difficult when there is too much available. The use of that information needs to be looked at closely. What do you as an historian keep and what do you **discard**?

13.1 Selecting relevant evidence

Let us take the question in Unit 12 'What is a London street bollard doing in the centre of Swanage?' The three pieces of evidence you were given to answer that question were all closely related and could all provide valuable clues to the answer. You had no choice but to use the three examples offered because they were the only ones available to you. However, if you had had a free hand, there were other available clues which you may, or may not have found useful. You would have to decide, for instance, if you would have found it useful to have a picture of Durham Cathedral. You were told in the description of Fig. 12.2 that Purbeck stone was used in the construction of the cathedral, so a picture of it could have been relevant. But would it have helped you answer the question about the bollard? I think not. Although Durham Cathedral was closely associated with the Dorset stone industry, it had nothing whatsoever to do with the bollards. But, alternatively, you may have found a picture of a bollard on a street corner in London useful so that you could possibly make the link between that site and the present one.

Now we know that there is a connection between London and Swanage, let us see what other evidence we can find. The question in Unit 12 was 'What is a London street bollard doing in the middle of Swanage?', now ask yourself whether an historian would consider the following three items relevant examples to help in answering that question. Remember, he already has the information from the three descriptions in Unit 10.

Example A Fig. 13.1
A photograph of a gilt fish weather-vane. It originally came from the Billingsgate fish market in London which was demolished in 1874. George Burt of Swanage won the contract to build the new market on the same site. He shipped the weather-vane back to Swanage to use on the new house he was building for his retirement.

Fig. 13.1

This is a good example of the link between Swanage and London, but I hope you agree it has little to do with our original question.

44

Fig. 13.2

Example B Fig 13.2
A picture of the Swanage Town Hall. A notice on the wall tells us that the outside wall of the building came from the Mercers' Hall in London. (A Mercer is a dealer in textiles or small items.) It was first erected in London after the Great Fire in 1666 and was designed by a pupil of Sir Christopher Wren, who built a great deal of the new capital.

When the Mercers' Hall was about to be rebuilt in 1880 they wished to keep the front, but they found it was so black with city dirt that it was cheaper to build a completely new one rather than have the original cleaned. George Burt acquired the **facade** and had it sent, stone by stone, to Swanage to its present site.

Again a very good example of the close tie between the capital and the coastal resort, but I do not think an historian would use it to answer the question.

SWANAGE TOWN HALL

THE 1670 A.D. FACADE
WAS BROUGHT FROM
MERCERS' HALL LONDON
AND ERECTED HERE 1882.

Plaque by Tithe Barn

Example C Fig. 13.3
This building now stands on the shore line at Swanage. Originally it was the Wellington Clock Tower built in London in 1854. By 1863 it was causing an obstruction to traffic, so it was declared a nuisance and put up for sale. George Burt's company offered to remove it. It was taken down carefully in 1867 and shipped to Swanage.

Fig. 13.3

The clock, originally situated where the round window now is, never came with it. The first tower had a spire but this was taken down in 1904 and replaced with the present top.

Does this example benefit our historian? I do not think so, but again it does show the close link between the two communities.

13.2 Relevance

So, not one of our examples would help us to answer the question, none of them gives any clue about why the bollards went to Swanage. We have read about other articles that have come from London, but not one of these mentions a bollard, the only thing they have in common as far as these examples and the bollards are concerned is that all came from the capital. **But** what if we now ask 'Which person played an important role in bringing parts of London to Swanage?' Give examples of these buildings. You would certainly use all the examples above and at least one from Unit 12.

Do you see how a change in question or a slight change in emphasis means that the material an historian is looking at changes its **significance**? Although the examples above were not at all suitable for the question about the arrival of the bollards in Swanage, they are ideal in helping to answer the second question.

Activities

Questions

1 Which person played an important role in bringing parts of London to Swanage? Give examples of these buildings and articles.

2 What other information would you have found useful in helping you to answer the question about the bollards in Unit 12?

3 (As you will see in a later unit, a photograph can show more than the photographer originally intended it to.) What is the small building in the bottom left-hand corner of Example C. What was it used for?

Summary

1 Do not throw away any notes or information you are given or find out for yourself; it may be unsuitable to help you with the topic you are doing at that particular time, but it could be very useful at another time, and by keeping the notes, you may save yourself a lot of research in the future.

2 Remember an historian must **discriminate** (choose) between the information that will be useful and that which will not.

Unit 14

Cause and effect

Much of what affects your life and the lives of other people is often caused by something else happening either in another time or even another place. Great, as well as simple inventions and ideas have occurred because man has always searched for something new to overcome a certain problem or to do a certain job, to make life easier.

14.1 Early developments in weapons

We can use a simple example to show how things have been invented or adapted to overcome certain problems.

Early man ate only what he caught by hunting or could gather from the wild vegetation. In the beginning the only weapons he had available were those lying on the earth around him. He had not yet learned to make these stones and sticks into sharper and more effective weapons, so all he could do was throw them at his intended prey.

But have you ever tried to throw a large stone over a long distance? If you have, you will know that it is not very easy.

Imagine the scene: you are hidden behind a rock, you are armed with small stones waiting for a deer to appear. After a long, patient wait, one comes into range. You quickly grab your stone, throw it... and miss. The deer has heard you, runs off and does not return. So you, and your family will now go hungry unless you manage to find some roots and berries on your way back to your shelter.

As you can see, the problem was that early man had to be extremely accurate with his stone-throwing if he was to have any chance of killing any big-game. His family relied on him catching these animals and if he did not they would then be close to starvation.

Traps

After many hundreds of years hunting in this way, man gradually realized that in order to catch animals he needed to slow them down in some way. If he could trap the animal he would be able to throw his stones at it more accurately and have a better chance of killing it and so his family would have a better chance of surviving. The simplest way of slowing down his victim was to dig a pit, cover it with vegetation to disguise it and then force the animal concerned to travel in the direction of the trap. Once it trod on the branches, they would give way and the victim would fall into the pit. Once it was in the trap, the men could stand around the edge and throw their rocks and stones on to the animal.

The spear

However, a deer is reasonably small, and although it would not have liked being trapped, it could do nothing but run around in the pit. It was of no danger to the hunter. But what would happen if a much larger animal, such as a mammoth, was caught. It would not be prepared to sit in the pit and wait to be killed, it would fling its trunk about and charge with its tusks so the men on the side would be in great danger and would often find themselves in the pit with the animal. Not a very pleasant prospect! What the men needed to do now was to find some method of throwing their stones accurately from a greater distance. The sticks and stones they were throwing separately were having little effect, but what would happen if they joined them together and sharpened them a little? By doing this they invented the spear. Now they could stay out of range of the flailing trunk and tusks, but still throw their weapons at the animal.

The bow and arrow

As man became more **proficient** at catching and killing his prey, the number of animals available in the immediate area decreased. Therefore, when food became scarce they were forced to travel greater distances to get it. If they were to be away for longer periods they needed to make sure that their journeys were worthwhile. They could not afford to travel for two or three days and return to their camp empty-handed, they needed a weapon which was more accurate than a rough spear, but at the same time able to kill the animal. They would not have time to dig pits to trap the animal, so they required a weapon which put more distance between the hunter and the hunted.

The natural progression from the spear was the mini-spear powered by a rough bow rather than thrown by hand – the bow and arrow. These were more accurate than the spear, and the men, now working in groups, could easily provide ample food for their families.

Inventions of necessity

A later development was to train wild dogs to round up and chase the herds of deer towards the hunters. In this way they could kill even more.

So these simple inventions: **stone** . . . **trap** . . . **spear** . . . **bow and arrow** . . . **training dog** . . . were all brought about by man's desire to eat and to support his family. He also invented new methods of carrying his food. At first he would have dragged the dead animal on the ground behind him, but if he had to travel any distance it would have become very messy and gritty by the time he got it home, and remember, he would have eaten it raw. Eventually he invented a simple framework of branches and leaves which he could pull behind him (very similar to that used by American Indians in cowboy films for carrying their wounded comrades back to camp). They called it a **travois**. Early man could also travel by water, putting his dinner over a log and floating it down river or later putting it in a dug-out canoe.

14.2 The pace of development

What you must remember is that these developments took place over a long period of time, often thousands of years. They did not happen overnight. All the new ideas had to pass from group to group by word of mouth and so the ideas took a long time to travel and they were often changed on the way when a group managed to find an easier way of doing things. The cause of all the changes in the example given was the desire to eat and, therefore, survive. If early man had not changed and adapted his ways he would have died out as a species.

We can trace these lines of development in many areas: the development of the aeroplane caused by the modern need to travel from A to B quickly. Space travel beyond our own planet enables man to explore the 'Last Frontier'. Car designers need to find a car which travels more miles for each gallon of petrol because the price of fuel is high and drivers want to own a more economical car. All these things have occurred because of some need. Today changes like these happen very quickly because, with modern communications systems, news and ideas can be transmitted more quickly.

But the further back in time, the longer it took for any changes to become known and take effect.

Activities

1 Draw a series of pictures showing the changes and the reasons for these changes in some aspect of history which interests you, for example, steam trains to diesel.

2 Can you think of another reason why the aeroplane developed quickly during this century? The years 1914 to 1918 and 1939 to 1945 may give you a clue.

Summary

1 Changes are often brought about for a **specific** reason e.g. early man needed to eat in order to survive. . . he could only eat what he could catch. . . therefore he had to change his methods of hunting to provide food for his family and his group.

2 Changes occur over a shorter period of time now because communications between people and countries are made faster by telephone, telex, television, computers and books.

3 Most historical changes were a response to some need; they did not just happen.

Unit 15

Primary sources

In the previous units we have been looking at different types of material. Some of it has been in the form of photographs, some you have gathered by asking your relatives, and some has been written work put together from a series of notes.

The historian has many such sources available to him, but some can be more useful than others, as we saw in Units 10 to 13. If he uses information that does not come from books i.e. that which he has gathered himself from his surroundings or from original documents or letters or carvings, he is using what are called **primary sources**. These are sources of information which are in their original form, they are **first hand**. (A list of these is given at the end of the unit.)

15.1 Definition of a primary source

An example of this type of material is as follows: you have written a diary and you have put parts of that diary into a history project at school: you have used a primary source of information. You were the person who wrote the diary and nobody else was involved. However, if you found another book in which extracts from someone else's diary had been described and, after putting it into your own words, you used this information in your history project, you would have used a **secondary source** of information, because someone else was involved before you. Whoever wrote the book, from which you gathered your information, has already completed all the hard work: he or she found the diary and extracted the facts from it. You are in fact taking notes from their work and not the diary, you are gaining the information **second hand**.

15.2 Secondary sources: drawbacks

It is useful to use first-hand sources because it provides the historian with original clues to work from. The possible problem with using second-hand or secondary material (and in some cases primary material) is that the historian may be influenced by the first writer's opinion or **bias**.

What is bias?

Imagine you are a great fan of a particular pop group. You are asked to write about your favourite pop group in an English lesson at school. Being a fan you will naturally write down all the good things about them; why they are good, their good sound, their fashionable clothes etc. Anyone reading your account would therefore have a very biased description of this group, because you may not have mentioned their bad habits and the way they treat their fans. If anyone used your work to write a similar account of their own, they would be influenced by what you have written, and consequently will not write a 'balanced' account, giving both the good and the bad points about the group.

15.3 Bias in primary sources

Some primary material may also be biased and the historian has to be careful when he uses any source. This will be fully explained in a later unit, but can you see the problem that could occur if the diary in our first example was written by a Frenchman during the wars against Britain in the early 1800s? Do you think he would give a good account of the British Army?

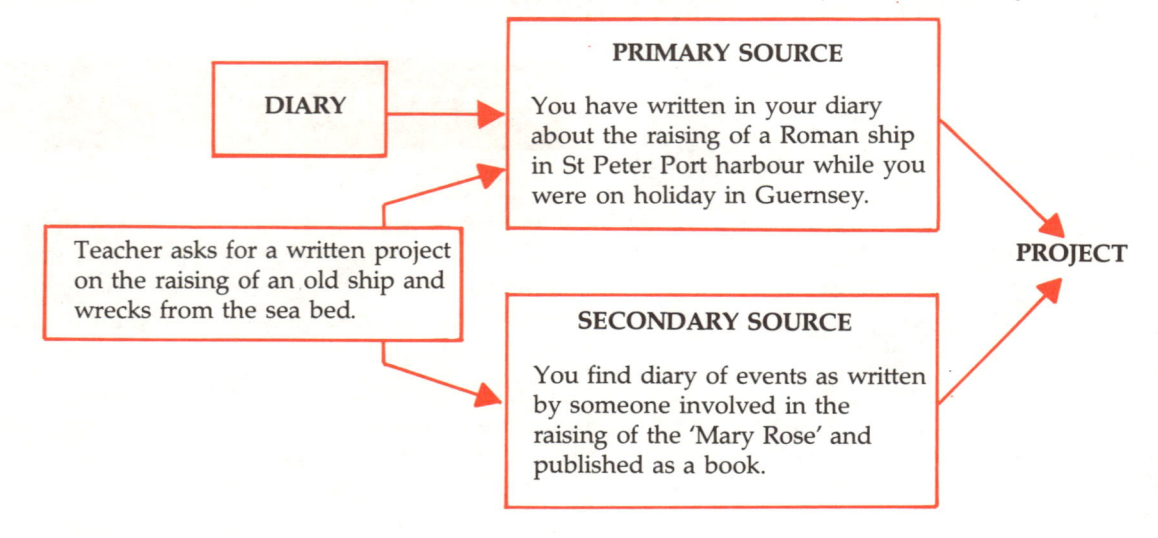

DIARY → **PRIMARY SOURCE** You have written in your diary about the raising of a Roman ship in St Peter Port harbour while you were on holiday in Guernsey. → PROJECT

Teacher asks for a written project on the raising of an old ship and wrecks from the sea bed.

→ **SECONDARY SOURCE** You find diary of events as written by someone involved in the raising of the 'Mary Rose' and published as a book. → PROJECT

('Le soldat anglais est barbare. Il détruit tout autour de lui – animaux moissons et maisons. Il préfere se remplir l'estomac que de combattre. Sa bravoure et son courage ne peuvent égaler ceux de nos glorieux lanciers. Nous ne pouvons pas perdre cette bataille, conduits par l'audace de notre Empereur. Vive la France.')

A French soldier's account 14 June 1815. 'The British soldier is a barbarian. He destroys everything around him, animals, crops and houses. He is more concerned with filling his stomach than with fighting. His bravery and courage do not compare with our glorious lancers. We cannot lose this battle under the audacious leadership of our Emperor. Long live France.'

The following units will look very closely at some different types of primary source material you are likely to come across in your studies. They will show you how to use these sources.

15.4 Examples of primary sources

Here is a list of some primary sources the historian may have access to. (Some of these are equally accessible to you, so you will be able to use some of them to provide you with information for your project in Volume 3.)

Letters
diaries/memoirs
   (A person's personal memories written down)
Photographs
Autobiographies
   (A story or history of a person actually written by that person)
Log book
church/parish record
   (Contains the baptisms, marriages and deaths within a parish)
Carved inscriptions on monuments, tombstones etc
Maps
Lists
Financial accounts
   (Showing how people spent and earned their money)
Any documents
Archaeological evidence
   Pottery, coins, statues, tools, skeletons, buildings, sites of buildings etc
Place names
   (Can give good clues about the original site or settlement)

There are many other sources of primary information and you can add them to this list as and when you find them.

Activities

Questions

1 Why would a French soldier not give a balanced account of the wars against Britain?
2 If you wanted to get a good account of these wars, what other material could help you?
3 Divide the following list into primary and secondary sources:

   School text books   Maps
   Autobiographies   History books
   Documents   Videotapes
   Hollywood movies   Carved inscriptions
   History journals   Church/parish registers
   Biographies   Letters

Summary

1 Primary source material provides information in its original form. It has not been changed by any other person.
2 When using any written or pictorial material the historian must be aware of **bias**.
3 When using primary sources it is useful, where possible, to know who wrote it or who took a particular photograph etc, so that you are aware of any possible bias.

Unit 16

The use of photographs

Throughout this book we have used many photographs to illustrate the units, and you are certain to come across many more in your study of history. But what do photographs actually show us and how can you, as an historian, **interpret** or explain the content of a photograph you find in a book or from a library?

In the project section of Volume 3 you will use photographs to illustrate your material. They will either be ones you have taken yourself or they might belong to other people, but whichever pictures you decide to use, you need to choose them carefully and they need to be relevant to the work you are doing.

16.1 Witting and unwitting testimony

But just how useful are photographs? There are two questions to ask yourself when you look at any photographic evidence: (a) What does the photographer want me to see in this picture? and (b) What else can I see in the picture that may be helpful to me as an historian?

The subject of the photograph that the photographer wants you to see is called the **witting testimony**. In other words, the main concern of the photographer taking the photograph was to show the viewer this particular subject, whatever it may be: a building, a person or scene of some sort. The part of the photograph the photographer was not especially interested in and which was not the main subject of the photograph is called the **unwitting testimony**; it just happened to be there. The photographer does not set out to take his photograph with the intention of showing this aspect to the viewer.

16.2 Unwitting testimony

There is an advantage in taking photographs yourself when doing any project or written work which requires photographic illustrations, because you know what you will see when they are developed, but even so they can often tell you more than you first realized.

For instance, if you take a snap of your brother or sister standing on a beach during your holiday, the main subject matter of the photograph is your brother or sister. This is the witting testimony: 'Here is my brother Jack on the beach at Bournemouth 1979.' But, unwittingly you are also showing the viewer other things e.g. what the weather was like – was your brother standing in the sunshine or was it raining? What the fashions were like in 1979 – what was your brother wearing? Were there any boats or cars in the picture? If so, what did they look like?

These and other details extracted from the photograph may not seem important to you now, but in a few years time you may look at this picture and laugh at the style of clothes and question the design of the cars. What information would a person gain if they came across this same photograph in a hundred years time?

A very practical example

Unwitting testimony in photographs was very useful to the planners of the Allied Invasion of Europe for 'D' Day 6 June 1944. During the planning an appeal appeared in the newspapers for any photographs or postcards of the North Atlantic coastline of France. Twenty thousand examples arrived in the first post, many of them simple holiday snap-shots. However, the 'unwitting' information they contained was extremely useful in deciding the best place to invade.

16.3 How to examine a photograph

Let us take some actual examples of photographic evidence and see how they could be of use to the historian. The process of **deduction** is the same whichever photographs you may use, the most important thing, however, is to look at the picture very carefully and examine all of it – not only that part which the photographer wishes you to see. Do not forget to ask yourself the two questions and see also Unit 17.

Look at Fig. 16.1. This is a photograph of the workers at a tin-box factory in the 1920s. The witting testimony i.e. what the photographer wanted the photograph to show is 'The Work Force', and in itself it is a very interesting photograph. However, what is more interesting to you as an historian is the unwitting testimony available i.e. what the photographer has shown without realizing it.

Look at the fashions. How many people can you see **not** wearing a hat? It seems they were very popular. You can see two types of hat in this picture, the flat cap seems to be fashionable for the men and the cloche hat for the ladies. Look at the ladies' coats; many have fur collars which suggests that they were the 'trendy' thing to wear in the 1920s. How many people can you see

Fig. 16.1 Workers at a tin-box factory in the 1920s

wearing spectacles? I am sure that not all these people had perfect eyesight so why do you think so few wore glasses?

Look at the difference in numbers between male and female workers; there seem to be far more women than men. This tells us that more women were employed in this industry than men – which suggests that perhaps the type of work was more suited to female labour. We could support this theory by finding other evidence, either photographic, or if we were very lucky, a wages book showing everybody's name and rate of pay.

Do you see how much information it is possible to find in such a photograph by examining it closely?

Activities

Look carefully at Fig. 16.2. What is the witting testimony in this photograph? In order to extract the unwitting testimony answer the following questions:

1. How many men can you see in the photograph?
2. The work force in this area of the factory is mainly male. True or False?
3. Accurately describe what the ladies are wearing.
4. Why are they wearing caps on their heads?
5. What is the power needed to work the machines on the left of the photograph?
6. What is the power needed to work the machines on the right of the photograph?
7. How is the factory lighted? (Look very closely.)
8. How many windows are there in the picture?
9. Can you see any signs of heating? What do you think working conditions would have been like in the winter?

Having extracted this information, write a paragraph with the title 'A description of a machine shop in a tin-box factory in the 1920s'. Use only the information you have gathered from answering the questions and what you can actually see in the picture.

If you do this properly you will have gained a lot of information from a photograph simply showing a factory scene. Can you see how useful the unwitting testimony can be? We will look at this again in Unit 17.

Summary

1. The information a photographer sets out to show in a photograph i.e. the main subject matter, is called the **witting testimony**.
2. The information provided in a photograph which is not necessarily the main subject matter is called the **unwitting testimony**.
3. Both witting and unwitting testimony is very useful to the historian.
4. An historian needs to examine photographs very carefully in order to extract all the information. Photographic evidence can be just as important as written evidence.

Fig. 16.2 A machine shop in a tin-box factory

Unit 17

Photographs: care in use

As well as using photographs as a source of information as we did in Unit 16, they are also useful, of course, for illustrating your own work. You have already been given various suggestions about how they could be used in previous units, but as with other information you need to choose the illustrations carefully. They must be relevant and have something to do with the subject you are working on. However, they do not need to be professionally produced photographs; you may not be able to find any.

17.1 Usefulness of unwitting testimony

We saw in Unit 16 how easy it was to extract unwitting testimony from photographs, and in the same way, you can find useful information from your family photograph album, especially if you are lucky enough to have one which goes back a number of years. These are particularly useful for showing not only those of your relatives who lived before you were born, but also what they were wearing and in some cases what jobs they did. If it is a picture outside a dwelling it will show you what the housing looked like at the time. All these facts and many more can be extracted with simple but careful examination of the photograph concerned. In Volume 3 you will be given instructions on how to produce your own project so, with that in mind, it would be useful to start searching at home for photographs of your family or perhaps asking your relatives if they have any you could borrow.

17.2 Authenticity of photographs

Having seen how useful photographs can be, let us look at what the historian needs to be careful of when using them. How do you know, as an historian, whether or not the photograph you are looking at is genuine? The two photographs in Unit 16 were staged ones. The photographer would come along, set up his camera, make the people pose and take the picture. Remember, he would not have had a small camera like those available today, it would have been a large plate-camera, difficult to carry and to assemble quickly. While he was taking the photograph the people would have to stand very still, otherwise they would have appeared as a blur on the printed picture.

A test of authenticity

In Unit 16 you were told to ask yourself two questions when looking at any photograph: what does the photographer want me to see in this picture, and what else can I see in the picture that may be helpful to me as an historian? Sometimes you also need to ask yourself a further question: where was the photographer standing when he took this photograph? Usually it does not matter where he was standing, but sometimes the accuracy of the photograph can be tested by working this out. For example, imagine during your search for photographic evidence for your project you find the picture of soldiers fighting in the First World War (Fig. 17.2).

The picture seems to be genuine and accurate. It shows what the soldiers were wearing and the equipment they were carrying, and you can see that the ground is bare and the conditions were not very good. Very useful, but look again. What if the soldiers were coming towards you? Where would the photographer have to be standing to take such a photograph – in the middle of the two armies. In our example the British soldiers have left their trenches and are advancing across the

Fig. 17.2

battlefield towards the photographer and the enemy. Remember, the photographer did not have a little camera he could keep in his pocket, he had a lot of equipment which required a long time to set up. So do you really think this particular photograph was actually taken on the battlefield?

I do not think any wartime photographer in World War One would have got himself between two groups of opposing soldiers and put himself in so much danger. A photograph like this would have been used for **propaganda** and could have been taken in a park in Paris or London, or in old trenches behind the front-line. The soldiers themselves may have been actors and just before the photograph was taken a few smoke canisters would have been set off to create the correct atmosphere. A photograph like this could still be useful to you because the unwitting testimony i.e. the uniforms and equipment would have been genuine but the witting testimony is not as valuable, because it is not genuine.

Activities

A second example can be seen in Fig. 17.3 which shows a group of British soldiers in Flanders during World War One. They are wearing masks on their faces to protect themselves from a German gas attack. But was this photograph really taken in a front line trench during a gas attack? Look at it carefully and then answer the following questions.

1 Where was the photographer standing when he took this photograph?

2 Do the soldiers' uniforms look as though the men have spent a long time in the muddy trenches of the Western Front?

If you have looked carefully you will have realized that the photographer must have been

Activities continued

Fig. 17.3

standing between the two armies, outside the protection of the trench during a gas attack. The uniforms look very clean, in fact too clean for soldiers at the front. Again this was probably a staged photograph to show the general public what precautions the British Army was taking against a gas attack. In fact, if you look closely there is a soldier in the background without a gas mask. This would have been printed in the newspapers in Britain to show the wives and girlfriends of the men fighting that all was being done to ensure their safety. As well as looking at the content of the photograph it is useful on some occasions for the historian to know the age of it, or the date it was taken. Not only does it give the content of the photograph a time scale, but it can also help to work out whether or not it is genuine. The camera was not invented until the 1840s and was a very expensive and rare article, so few photographs were taken until the late 1800s and then only by those people who could afford to own one. (Therefore any photograph dated before 1850 should be very carefully investigated.)

Summary

1 Photographs can be very useful for illustrating your own work.

2 Sometimes you need to ask yourself where the photographer was standing when he took the picture in order to question its accuracy.

3 Cameras were very rare, very expensive and bulky before 1900. They took a long time to set up, so it was difficult to take many pictures.

4 Remember there will be a project section in Volume 3 dealing with your family and/or your local area. It would be worthwhile starting to collect material, photographic or written, which you consider would be useful for your own project work.

Revision Units 16 and 17

Practice with photographs

In this revision unit you will see four photographs. In order to extract the relevant information answer the following questions. Some of them require more examination than others and some will require you to look at some of the photographs in Units 1 to 17.

IN A COTTAGE ON THIS SITE, THE REV. JOHN WESLEY STAYED 12-13 OCTOBER 1774. THE COTTAGE WAS DESTROYED BY ENEMY ACTION 14 MAY 1941

Fig. R1

1. Fig. R1
(a) Who was the Reverend John Wesley mentioned on this plaque?
(b) In which year did he stay at this cottage in Dorset?
(c) The plaque tells us that the cottage was destroyed by enemy action in 1941, who was the enemy?

2. Fig. R2
(a) What do you think is the witting testimony in this photograph?
(b) What is the job of the lady in white? How do you know?
(c) How is this room lighted, is the lamp electric or gas?
(d) What does the cabinet on the wall contain?
(e) What is there in this photograph that would help you work out the approximate year it was taken? (Clue: to find the answer you may have to look at a book of fashion.)
(f) How does this medical room differ from a modern one?
(g) What is the first impression you get about the room in this photograph?

Fig. R2

Revision

3. Fig. R3
   (a) How many horses can you see in this picture?
   (b) What is the man wearing?
   (c) What is the wall on the left made of?
   (d) What is the connection between Figs. R3 and R4. (Write at least five lines.)
   (e) What is the link between Figs. R3 and R4, and Fig. 12.1?
   (f) Is the horse and cart in this photograph the witting or unwitting testimony?

Fig. R3

Fig. R4

4. Fig. R4
   (a) This is a genuine photograph taken in 1810. True or False? Give reasons for your answer.
   (b) Using the information from the photograph can you explain how the crane on the left is controlled?
   (c) What is the crane being used for?
   (d) Write down **five** examples of unwitting testimony in this photograph?
   (e) Describe the character in this picture whom you consider to be the most important.

General
(a) Without turning back to the previous pages write down the two questions an historian must always ask himself when examining photographs.
(b) What question can you ask when not sure of the accuracy of the picture?
(c) How do you know that the photographs showing the fighting in World War One were not actually taken on the battlefield?
(d) What does the word **propaganda** mean?
(e) Why did people have to stand perfectly still when having their photographs taken in the early part of this century?
(f) Write down a list of possible places where you could find photographs that may be useful to you in your project in Volume 3.

Unit 18

Diaries

Do you own a diary? If you do, what do you write in it? People use them for different reasons: some use them to plan their events and meetings for the coming week or year, some carry specialist diaries which provide them with useful advice on their hobbies and interests, and some write down everything that happened to them each day, what they ate, where they went and what type of day they had.

For example:

> **Mon 22 June 1972**
> *Woke as usual 6.30 a.m. Very wet and windy. Had breakfast and left for the office at 7.45 a.m. Traffic bad. Road works on M4 caused traffic-jams so arrived late at the office. Miss Simms in Accounts ill so no finance meeting today. Had early lunch in new pub, 'Wee Waif', interesting people. Food good, but expensive. Sunny at lunchtime. Coffee machine in office broken again, no drinks. Left office early and played a few holes of golf before returning home. Weather improved throughout the day. Cannot watch the cricket tonight on the TV because it was rained off!!*

18.1 Extracting information

This diary entry for 1972 tells us quite a lot about the life of the writer. Use the following questions to extract the relevant information.

1. What time does this person get up every morning?
2. Write down a weather forecast for Mon 22 June 1972 (from the extract above).
3. This person has two interests which he mentions. What are they?
4. On this particular day what was his journey to work like?
5. Did he usually travel to work by train, if not how do you know?
6. Who was ill? What was cancelled because of this absence?
7. Where did he go for lunch? What did he think of it?
8. Is this the first time that the coffee machine has broken?
9. Apart from the date, what other evidence is there in this extract that tells you it was written recently. Why could it not have been written in the 1920s?
10. In no more than ten lines, and using only the information available to you, describe the writer of this extract: his work, interests etc.

18.2 Diaries as personal account

Diaries like these give the reader a very interesting picture of what life was like at the time they were written. This is why so many people find it fascinating to read other peoples' diaries. They are usually very personal documents, and unlike general history books, give a description of life through the eyes and experience of one individual. If you write your own diary you are in fact cataloguing some of your own personal history. When you read it again in years to come you will not only be reminded of the events you wrote about now but also of what life in general is like today. You would then be able to compare your lifestyle over a long period of time.

18.3 Famous diarists

There are some very famous diarists who have written down their everyday experiences. You have probably heard of Samuel Pepys (1633 to 1703). He wrote his diary in code so that only he could read it and so the contents would remain secret. However, when the code was broken the diary revealed a great deal about the time of King Charles II, including the Plague of 1665, and the Great Fire of 1666. Also it tells the reader about his own personal life, what he ate, the clothes he wore, how he felt, a description of his house and servants and many other things of interest to the historian.

Another diarist who has become very famous recently is **Edith Holden**. She lived from 1871 to 1920 and in her diary she described the very ordinary things of life, the flowers, the trees and animals throughout the seasons of the year. Her diary has become so popular with the public that not only has it become a bestseller, but the illustrations contained in it have appeared as designs on china, curtain material, wallpaper and even saucepans.

Not all diarists have been adults. The diary of **Anne Frank**, written when she was only thirteen, tells the very moving story of how she and her family hid from the Germans in Amsterdam during World War Two and the day-to-day problems they faced.

Unit 18 continued

Fig. 18.1 Samuel Pepys, the famous diarist. You will learn more about him in Unit 19.

18.4 Care in use

The historian can use diaries like any other source of information, but he does need to remember that he is reading only one person's point of view. Comments written in diaries can often be very biased and affected by how the writer is feeling at the time. We all get angry and upset on occasions about things which happen to us. Most people forget about them very quickly, or talk about them to other people. Some, however, write down these events in their diaries and because of their anger the description can be different from what actually happened. Someone reading this account at a later date would not be reading a true account of what actually happened, for example:

> **'Wed 8 Dec**
> *Crashed the car. Some idiot hit the side of me as I was coming out of the Brafford Junction. Should have been looking where he was going. Was travelling much too fast. Needs his lights fixed as well, I couldn't see him.'*

The writer in this example has been involved in an accident. He is naturally angry. In his diary he has put all the blame on the other driver. Do you think the other driver was entirely to blame? What is there in this extract to suggest that perhaps the writer was at fault? If the other driver wrote down his experience it would probably describe the exact opposite to the above. They would both be personal descriptions of the same event. When reading a diary you, as an historian, must remember that you are looking at a personal view of an event or a series of events which was usually never meant to be read by anyone other than the writer. We will look at a specific diary in Unit 19 and see how useful it can be to an historian.

Activities

In a notebook, or in a proper diary, if you have one, keep a record of all the things you do, see and experience in the coming week. Be as accurate as possible so that you can use the information at a later date. If possible ask your mother or father to keep a diary for the same period of time and see how they differ at the end of the week. Read also Units 19 to 21.

Summary

1 Diaries can give the historian two types of information – a description of an actual event, e.g. Samuel Pepys and the Great Fire, and a description of everyday life at the time of writing. The second type of information is just as, and often more, important than the first.

2 A diary entry is only one person's view of an event. Usually it is not meant to be read by anyone other than the writer himself.

3 Remember accounts in diaries are often biased, therefore, an historian must remember this when using a diary as a source of information.

Unit 19

The diary of Samuel Pepys

In Unit 18 we mentioned the famous diarist Samuel Pepys. His diaries have been used a great deal by historians studying the period of time between 1 Jan 1600 and 31 May 1669. This was the time Pepys was writing about and it was a very important period in English history because it saw the return of a King – Charles II in 1660, (after eleven years of rule by Parliament, Oliver and Richard Cromwell), the Plague of London in 1665 and the Great Fire of London in 1666. But Pepys also gives the reader of his diaries an important look at home life of the time. He was a well-paid man in a high position, so we only see the best side of life, but, nonetheless, it is a great source of information about how the wealthy lived.

19.1 Extracts on home life

There is a vast quantity of material contained in all his diaries, so the following are only small samples of the information in them, but even these few extracts can give the reader useful first-hand facts.

First of all what does he tell us about his home life?

26 January 1660
'Home from my office to my Lord's lodgings where my wife had got ready a very fine dinner; a dish of fowl, three pullets and a dozen larks all in a dish, a great tart, a neat's tongue, a dish of anchovies, a dish of prawns and cheese. My company was my father, my uncle Fenner, his two sons, Mr Pierce, and all their wives and my brother Tom.

What a feast! But this extract tells us more than just that Mr Pepys ate well. It also gives us the names of some of his friends and relatives, their relationship to him and the fact that they were all married.

Pepys however, did not always eat like this; an entry in the diary for 4 April 1664 says 'Home, and being washing day, dined on cold meat.'

We also discover some hygiene problems he experienced:

31 May 1662
'Had Sarah to comb my head clean, which I found to be so foul with powdering and other troubles, that I am resolved to try, how I can keep my head dry without powder; and I did in a sudden fit cut off all my beard, which I had been a great while bringing up, only that I may with my pumice stone do my whole face as I do now with my chin which I find a very easy way, and gentle.'

It was common for the wealthy to powder their hair. They also had a lot of trouble with headlice which had to be washed or combed out.

He also informs the reader how much he paid his staff, and what he thought of it.

26 March 1663
'This morning came a new cooks-maid at £4 per annum (per year), the first time I ever did give so much.'

This cooks-maid seemed to be well paid according to Pepys' standards, but she only earned £4 per year and we know from later entries that one month he spent £55 on clothes.

Apart from life at home, Pepys also describes life outside. It seems that fights in the streets were common at the time as he tells us on:

26 July 1664
'Great discussion today about the fray yesterday in Moorfields, how the butchers at first did beat the weavers, between whom there hath been ever an old competition for mastery, but at the last the weavers rallied and beat them. At first the butchers knocked down all the weavers that had blue or green aprons, till they were fain to pull them off and put them in their breeches. At last the butchers were fain to pull off their sleeves that might not be known and were soundly beaten out of the field and some deeply wounded and bruised.'

Also the theatre was a very popular pastime but was not always to Pepy's liking:

29 September 1662
'To the Kings Theatre, where we saw 'Midsummer Night's Dream' which I had never seen before, nor shall I ever again, for it is the most insipid, ridiculous play that ever I saw in my life.'

From other entries in the diaries it is obvious that he was not too keen on Shakespeare.
Pepys even tells us the time he stayed awake to write these diaries:

16 January 1660
'I staid up till the bellman came by with his bell just below my window as I was writing of this very line, and cried "Past one of the clocke, and a cold, frosty, windy morning".'

What information therefore can the historian gain from these few extracts dealing with his personal life? The following questions will help guide you towards the relevant information.

19.2 Extracts on public disasters

As well as having entries dealing with his home life and the sights around him, Pepys diaries also have a very serious side to them. His description of the Plague which swept through London in 1665 is very useful in plotting the progress of the disease through the city, but, unfortunately, is too detailed to mention here in full. The following extracts, however, provide enough evidence to show that life in London at the time was not at all pleasant.

31 August 1665
'Thus the month ends with great sadness upon the publick, through the greatness of the plague everywhere. Every day sadder and sadder news of its encrease. In the city (of London) died this week 7496 and of them 6042 of the plague. But it is feared that the true numbers of the dead is near 10 000...

Fig. 19.1 This grim scene was all too common during the plague years. It shows the unceremonious burial of victims in a makeshift grave

Unit 19 continued

He also tells us about the more human and touching scenes which occurred:

3 September (Lord's Day)
'Alderman Hooker told us of a child of a very able citizen in Gracious Street, a saddler, who had buried all the rest of his children of the Plague, and himself and wife now being shut up in despair of escaping, did desire only to save the life of this little child, and so prevailed to have it received stark-naked into the arms of a friend, who brought it, having put it into new fresh clothes, to Greenwich.'

Can you imagine what this saddler felt like having to give away his only child in order to save it, at the same time knowing that he and his wife were dying?

This type of extract shows why diaries can be important to the historian. You would be unlikely to find the information above in a general history book dealing with this period, except perhaps in a general sentence, e.g. 'Some people were forced to give away their children in order to save their lives.' But few would record it in the same way as this diary entry; a first-hand account of what happened by someone who was actually there at the time. We also get a good idea of Pepys' personal feelings about the Plague from various entries in the diary.

14 September 1665
'To hear that poor Payne my waiter, hath buried a child and is dying himself. To learn that a labourer I sent but the day to Dagenham, to know how they did there, is dead of the plague; and that one of my watermen that carried daily, fell sick as he landed me on Friday morning last, and is now dead of the plague. And lastly that both my servants, W. Hewer and Tom Edwards, have lost their fathers of the plague this week, do put me into great apprehension of melancholy and with good reason.'

The extract above needs no explanation, Pepys' sadness is expressed in the words. Many of the plague-infested houses of 1665 were destroyed in the Great Fire of London in 1666. The fire started in a baker's shop in Pudding Lane and quickly spread throughout the city. Most of the houses were wooden and had all been coated with pitch in order to preserve the timbers, so once they were alight they burnt immediately. Pepys provides an accurate and detailed description of both the fire and how it affected him personally.

3 September 1666
'Into Moorfields, our feet ready to burn, walking through the town among the hot coals, and find that full of people and poor wretches carrying their goods there . . .'

Fig. 19.2 The chaos of the Great Fire

5 September 1666

'About four o'clock in the morning, my Lady Batten sent me a cart to carry away all my money, and plate, and best things to Sir W. Ryders at Bednall Green, which I did, riding myself in my night gown in the cart.'

Pepys must have provided a very funny sight riding on a cart in his night gown!

7 September 1666

'Up by five o'clock and by water to Pane's Wharf. Walked thence and saw all the towne burned, and a miserable sight of Paul's Church with all the roofs fallen, and the body of the quire fallen into St. Fayths.'

The destruction of St Paul's Cathedral, even then one of the best churches in Europe, as described by a very tired Samuel Pepys. Later in the same day we learn that he stopped at a friend's house and borrowed a clean shirt and went to a meeting at St James's Palace.

All these examples, and countless others, in the diary, are useful to all historians studying these years. Some are sad, some humorous and some extremely descriptive. But what is important is that they give the reader a personal description of what life was like at the time, by someone who was actually there at the time.

19.3 The problem of bias

Remember, however, that this diary was of course written by only one man, and the fact that it was written in code tells us that the entries were not meant to be read by anyone except the writer. Therefore, they are very much one person's point of view and so some of the comments about people and places and events could be biased. We must read the entries with this in mind, and if they were used in a study of some kind, the events described would have to be supported by other historical material wherever possible. However, having said that, diaries written in such detail as these are rare and, therefore, provide more facts than the normal written material of the time.

Activities

1. Pepys on home life

(a) What was the name of Pepys' uncle?
(b) What was the name of Pepys' brother?
(c) What is a 'Neat's Tongue'?
(d) Why should wash day mean that Pepys had to eat cold meat?
(e) How did wealthy people of Pepys' time dry their heads? What problem did they have with their hair?
(f) Pepys' clothes for one month cost him £55. For how many years could he have paid his new cooks-maid with this amount?
(g) What item on his dinner table would you certainly not see today?
(h) Between whom was the fight?
(i) Why did the butchers take off their sleeves?
(j) Where did the fight take place?
(k) Where did Pepys go to the theatre?
(l) What words tell us that he was not impressed with the play he saw?
(m) Apart from the time, what other information did the bell-man supply?
(n) What was the time when Pepys wrote the entry on 16 Jan 1660?
(o) What impression about Pepys, the man, do you get from these examples? How did he live? What were his pastimes? What was his home life like?

2. Pepys on public life

(a) Why do you think there was a saddler in the centre of the city?
(b) What was the name of Pepys' waiter?
(c) What transport did Pepys use every day during the plague? How do you know?
(d) Why did the wooden houses burn quickly during the Great Fire?
(e) In the extract from 3 Sept 1666. Pepys mentions the words 'money and plate'. What is plate?
(f) Which architect was later responsible for the rebuilding of St Paul's Cathedral and much of the new city of London?
(g) Why is Pepys' diary so important to the historian?

More Activities

Further work

Using either the entry for 7 September 1666 or 3 September 1665 draw a picture to illustrate it.

There was another famous diarist writing at the same time as Pepys. Try to find out his or her name.

Unit 20

Letters

If you wish to send a message to a friend in the next town or village, how do you do it? Today you would probably use a telephone. The conversation between you and your friend would be both private and **confidential** and nobody else would be aware of what you said and no written notes would be taken. Telephone conversations are, therefore, of little use to the historian. But, how would you have delivered your message, or spoken to your friend before the invention of the telephone? Like many other people you would have written the message down on a piece of paper, and from the year 1840, you would have posted it for the price of one old penny then, to 17p today (1985).

20.1 Importance of letters to the historian

As far back as the Middle-Ages there were messengers all over the country whose job it was to carry government documents, riding along the main roads and changing horses every few miles. The important thing, however, is not that the post was delivered by messenger, on horseback or even by a modern postman in a van, but that the messages themselves were **written** down on paper. This is important because if these and other letters have survived and are in libraries and museums or in private houses, they can still be read and the information they contain can be very useful, especially to the historian.

They can provide him with facts about everyday life as well as important messages. However, as with the use of diaries in Unit 19, you must, as an historian, remember two important things:

1 The letters were usually written by individual people in private and were, therefore, not meant to be read by anyone other than the person receiving the letter.

2 The writing in the letters may be very **biased**. The information and comments they contain are only one person's, i.e. the writer's, point of view.

The advantage is, however, that sometimes they can give us a very honest view of what life was like at a time when people were possibly not always willing to speak about their personal feelings, but were able, as with the diary writer, to write down these feelings and comments in the form of a letter.

Different types of letter

Of course, not all letters that have been found have been pleasant ones, from one friend to another. Some of them deal with legal arrangements or the buying and selling of houses or land or other items. Some are letters of complaint and some describe events that were taking place at the time the letter was written.

Activities

Start at home

Where do you as an historian find the letters which can provide you with useful information? The easiest place to start is in your house or in your grandparents' house. **But** do not forget **all** letters are **private** so you must ask permission from your relatives before searching for, and certainly before reading, any letters you may find.

Assuming you have **permission**, where do you start? The simplest thing to do is to ask your relatives if they have any letters they think you might find interesting and which you may read. Asking may save you a lot of searching. Letters take up very little space on their own so it would be worth looking at the back of any drawer that looks as though it may contain papers of some kind. If the house has an attic you may find letters stored away in a shoe-box or something similar.

Going further afield

But where do you go if your search reveals no letters of interest? Your local museum, library or records' office may have collections of them, and even if they have none at all, they would be able to tell you where you could find some. If you have to go to such places to find your material it is worth working out beforehand the type of letters that you require: do you need examples of general letters of a certain time in history, or do you require business or legal letters or those of a particular individual or local personality? If you just arrive and ask if they have any letters you could use as a source of information, they may not be able to help you immediately and they will certainly ask **you** what type of information or letters you actually need.

What can you learn?

What type of letters can you hope to find and how useful are they? Usually at home you will come across those written from one member of your family to another. These may contain general conversation about many things, but could also provide you with useful facts about the relationships in your family in the past. Names may be mentioned which you have not heard of before and it may cause you to trace a larger family tree or change the time-line you did in Unit 4 to see where everyone fits into the family pattern.

You may also find letters or cards written from a holiday resort. These will provide you with information about what people did on their holidays and also perhaps what facilities were available to the holidaymaker in the past. If it is a picture postcard you will also see what the resort was actually like at that time.

You may be lucky enough to find a First World War postcard sent from France. Some of these had a particular message embroidered in silk thread on them. These are worth a lot of money today, so if you do find one, look after it carefully. Some were ordinary postcards which contained a type-written message. The men at the battle-front had to cross out the words they did not want. These cards were meant to stop the people at home in England worrying about their menfolk in the trenches, but they did not say much and often arrived at their destination long after they had been sent, and so the message could have changed.

Dear Betty,

I am well / unwell

I am wounded / not wounded

I hope to see you soon

Signed

The type of letter you may find more difficult to understand will be those containing legal arrangements of some kind. If you do find one of these, it would be better if you gave it to an adult who may be able to 'translate' it for you.

All letters are useful in one way or another, but if you find a lot of them, you will need to discriminate and sort out those you need and those you do not. However, if you do not require all of them now, you may do so at a later date so keep all of them in a safe place, or if you cannot keep them yourself keep a record of where you can find them again.

We will look at another possible place where you can find useful and interesting letters in Unit 21.

Summary

1 Remember that letters were written by individuals and were meant to be read only by the person receiving them.

2 Letters, like diaries, contain personal comments and points of view which may be biased.

3 All letters are private so make sure you obtain permission before you search for and read any letters.

4 Most letters are useful to you in some way or another. Whether you use a particular letter or not depends on the type of information you require for a topic or project. You must discriminate.

Unit 21

Letters in newspapers

In Unit 20 you were given examples of various places where you could look in the hope of finding letters which could provide you with certain information. As well as those already suggested, another place for you to look would be the letter columns of newspapers.

So far we have considered only letters from the past, but modern letters can be just as important because they are dealing with living history, as it happens. Some also refer back to times that the writer has lived through himself. (You will see an example of one such letter below.)

21.1 Letters in local newspapers

The letters which appear in the national newspapers often deal with questions and topics raised in earlier editions and are not usually very useful as a source. Local papers, however, often run series of articles dealing with the history of the local area. (These articles can also be very useful to you and we will look more closely at them in a later unit.)

The newspapers also often invite local people to write about their own experiences and memories. Other people who read the articles write letters to the newspaper concerned stating another point of view or disagreeing with the original writer's information. As you will see in the example, these types of letters can provide interesting facts which may be useful to you if you are doing a local project of some kind.

This letter written by Mr G. Lilley, was found in my local newspaper and it is an excellent example of the type of letter written in reply to such a series of articles. The letter contains some very interesting facts about a local industry within the town in which he lives. **But** remember when reading it that it does also contain a lot of **biased** comments because it is only Mr Lilley's memories and thoughts that are recorded.

'Sir,
I was not born in your town, but I have lived here since I was fifteen. I also worked from 1932–1936 at the well-known local factory mentioned by your previous writer, but, unlike him I have no cosy memories of that experience.

I see the crowds of men and women on foot and cycles hurrying towards the gates of the factory where the blue-uniformed watchmen stood while above us the cracked bell sounds urging the laggards on before the gates closed at 8.00 a.m.

I hear the trams clanging and whistling along the road disgorging from hard seats more and more workers, mostly shabbily dressed, the older men with crossed black scarves round their necks hiding the absence of a collar. I smell the stench of the cloakroom where the men changed their boots and put on greasy white coats and long white aprons. I also smell the ovens and the flour and the baking and the fires and oil from the machines. I see the long rooms with their ancient black machines pounding in continuous rhythm and hear again the slip-slap of the overhead belts.

I hear too the bored girls singing in unison the familiar songs of the thirties and hear their shrieks as they try to be heard over the noise of the machines.

Parties of people came round and looked at the workers as though they were animals in a zoo. There was a class-distinction too. Apart from on the sports field the office workers rarely mixed with the factory workers and to be a factory girl was considered to be the lowest one could get.

A few weeks ago I walked across the empty space where the factory had once been. I did not shed a single tear.

Yours faithfully,

G. Lilley'

This is an excellent example of a simple letter providing a great deal of possibly useful information. You can almost see the factory workers arriving to work in the morning, hurrying towards the factory before the gates closed and you can smell the product and the machinery in the rooms. But again, remember, this is only one man's point of view.

Extracting all the information

Just how useful is a letter of this kind? We know that it is biased, but even so there is a lot in it which could help you in a local project. It could at least provide you with a starting point for further study.

What information does it actually give us? Answer the following questions to help you decide. Some of the questions require a little more thought than usual!

(a) During which years did he work in the factory?
(b) What is there in the letter which gives a hint of **class-discrimination**?
(c) How did the workers come to work?
(d) How do we know that most of them were poor?
(e) Why were they wearing scarves?
(f) What do you think the factory made? Why have you chosen this answer?
(g) Is Mr Lilley the first person to write to the newspaper about this factory? How do you know?
(h) What did the men wear inside the factory?
(i) What were the overhead belts mentioned in the letter used for?
(j) Describe the girls in the factory.
(k) How do we know that Mr Lilley did not enjoy working in this factory?
(l) How do we know that he was not a local boy?
(m) Does this letter differ from the first one sent to the paper? What do you think that first one may have said?

Fig. 21.1 Workers travelling by tram in Bristol in the 1920s

(n) Make a list of the points in the letter which show it was **not** describing the present day.

You see that in this letter we get information not only about the actual factory, but we also get some idea of this individual's feelings. Letters provide us with a personal view of day to day and past events and they can be useful.

Activities

1 Read the letter again and using the description from one paragraph draw a picture to illustrate it. Try to put into your picture what Mr Lilley put into words. Try to make your drawing as accurate as possible. You may need to find out about the fashions of the time or what trams looked like.

2 In Volume 3 you will be asked to do a project of some kind. One of the example titles will deal with a local topic. It would be a very useful exercise to start reading through your local paper, if you have one, and collect any article or letter that you think you may be able to use with this topic.

3 Mr Lilley's letter is written from a worker's point of view. Using the same information, write down a description of a similar scene from the point of view of a manager at the same factory.

Unit 22

Personal records and documents

In Unit 21 we suggested that in order to find old written material i.e. letters and diaries from which you could gain information about your family, you searched (after having asked permission to do so) likely hiding places in your house. As well as finding letters, you are almost certain to come across or be given, a lot of documents and personal records dealing with various aspects of your family life. If you are lucky, it is sometimes possible to trace all the important events of one or more of your relative's lives by using all the documents referring to them and extracting the relevant information.

Such documents could include birth certificates, ration cards, school reports, national service papers, apprenticeship forms etc. In the project section of Volume 3, when you will study your family in more detail, we will take a very close look at some of these documents and see how they can be used effectively. In this unit you will be given some examples of the simple type of document you may find in your searches and you will be shown how easy it is to extract useful or required information.

22.1 Birth certificates

The most common document to start with is one that almost everybody has, even if they are only a few days old – a birth certificate. In England there are two types of certificate issued: a short certificate, which shows only basic information and a long certificate which can supply the

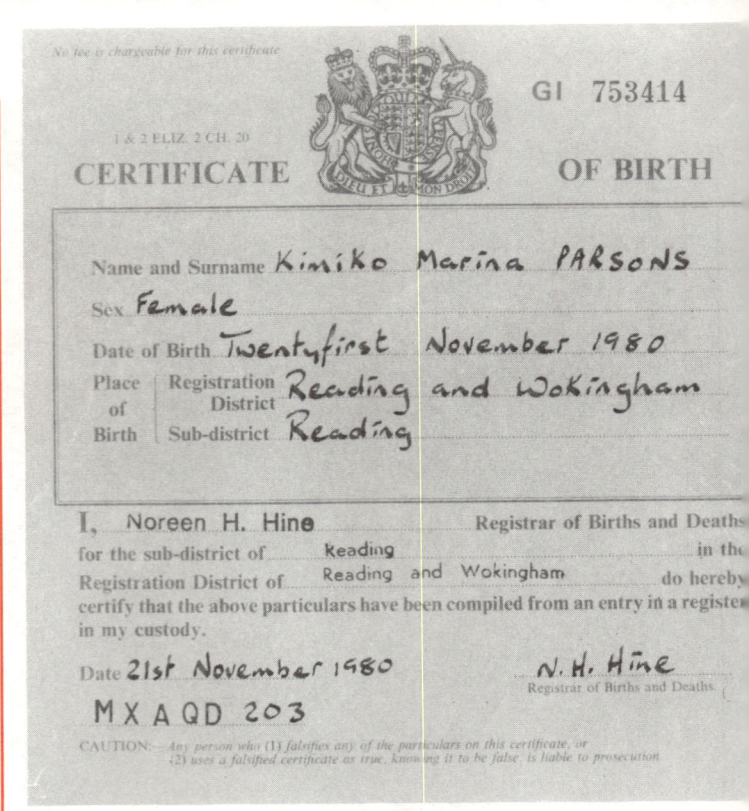

Fig. 22.1

historian with more facts, not only about the individual concerned but also about his or her parents.

Here are examples of each type of English birth certificate.

Fig. 22.1 shows a short certificate that gives only the name or names of the person being registered, the sex of the child, the actual date of birth (which is often different from the date the birth was registered), and the area or sub-district in which the registration took place. It is signed by the Registrar of Births and Deaths for that area; he is responsible for making sure that all the details on the certificate are correct and that they are kept safe in the register itself. (The number on the left indicates where the information on this certificate appears in the register.)

Fig. 22.2 shows a long certificate. It provides the reader with a lot more information than Fig. 22.1. Not only does it give the registration number, the date and place of birth, as well as the name and sex of the child, but also, as you can see, the full

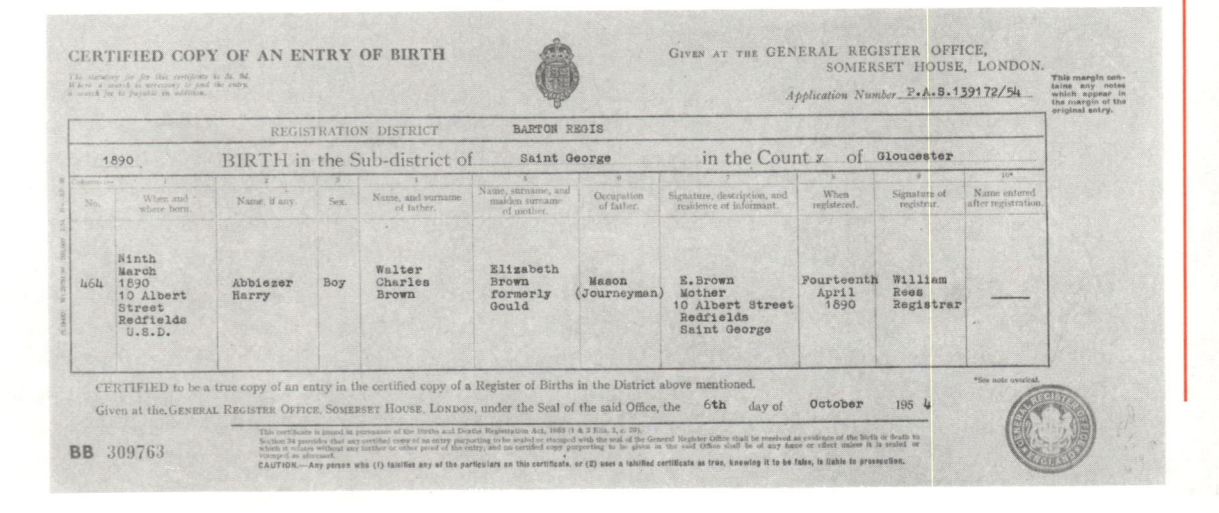

Fig. 22.2

names of the father and mother, including the mother's maiden name (the surname she used before she was married). It also gives us the rank or profession of the father. Again it is signed by the Registrar and so gives the reader an indication of where the registration took place, which could be useful if you wished to trace the person mentioned on it. (NB The person to whom this birth certificate belongs was born in 1890, but you will notice that it was registered in 1954. This is because the first certificate of 1890 was lost and this is a copy.)

From 1 July 1837, all births, as well as marriages and deaths, in England and Wales were supposed to have been registered. The indexes where you find the references to all the registrations can be found at St Catherine's House in the Aldwych, London. (In Volume 3 you will be shown how to obtain the relevant information you require from these registers.)

Birth certificates are therefore very useful documents especially if you are **researching** your own, or somebody else's family history. The information is usually clearly labelled and easily extracted as long as you can read the handwriting on the document! They are also very useful as a starting point for further study as you will see in a later unit.

22.2 Marriage certificates

The other personal documents which you may find at home and consider useful for your studies are marriage certificates and death certificates. (Copies of both types are also kept on file at St Catherine's House and can be purchased if you follow the correct procedure. This will be dealt with in Volume 3.)

As you will see in Fig. 22.3 a marriage certificate, given to the married couple on the day of their wedding, provides the historian with more details than just the names of the two people married and when and where the ceremony took place. It informs you, as the historian, of the age of the couple when they were married, what jobs they had, and where they lived immediately before the wedding. It also provides you with a description of their fathers' jobs. It is signed by the couple themselves, witnesses to the ceremony, and by the person who conducted it. The number on the left is the reference number of this entry in the parish registers.

A certificate like this may be of little historical interest to you if the people married are still

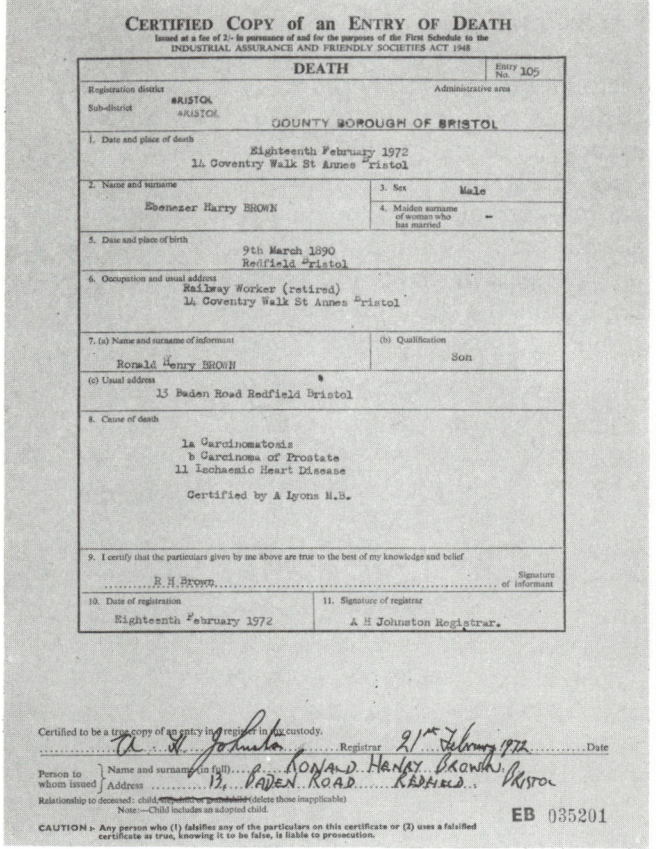

Fig. 22.4 A death certificate

alive, because you could probably get the same information by simply asking them, but it could prove to be a very important document if they are dead, or if you wanted to follow up the information on it to help you trace a member of your family with whom you had lost contact. It would give many starting points for continued research: the place of the wedding, the wife's/husband's name, occupation and their address. By checking on these details you may come across other clues and facts to explore.

Fig. 22.3

Unit 22 continued

Birth certificates, marriage certificates and death certificates are all legal documents. They are issued by someone in authority because they are required by law to do so, therefore, because each household should have at least one or two examples of them they should be relatively easy to find. However, there are many other simple types of personal document which are not necessarily kept by all families. Below are some simple examples of personal **documentation** which you may find in your searches. Some have only general interest value, an item which in itself, tells the historian very little, but they can provide a starting point for further study.

Fig. 22.5(a)

Fig. 22.5(b)

22.3 Documentation from war years

The document in Fig. 22.5 is one that you may find easily, but it was something that people often threw away when it was no longer required, so you may have to ask a number of your relatives who lived in the 1940s before you locate one to study. It is a **national registration identity card**. In 1939 a national register of all citizens in the British Isles was **compiled**. People were given a card and a personal registration number. This card had to be carried at all times and had to be shown to a uniformed police officer or a uniformed member of the armed forces on duty, if they demanded to see it. If the person named on the card moved house or district, the card had to be stamped and signed at the local national registration office. It was one way of keeping a check on the movement of the population and because they had to be shown before **ration books** were issued, it meant that foreign undesirables such as spies and secret agents would find it difficult to move around the country easily.

This particular example shows the name of the person to whom it was issued, plus her registration number, but more importantly it informs us that this lady moved twice from her original address. A useful fact if you were now trying to trace this person. You have three addresses which could give you a good starting point in your investigations. If Miss Brown no longer lives at Foxhill Rd, and the chances are that she does not, because the registration stamp says August 1950, neighbours there may remember either the place that she actually moved to or to which area she went. Your search would then have to start again at that point.

Fig. 22.5 (a) and (b) cover and inside of a national registration identity card

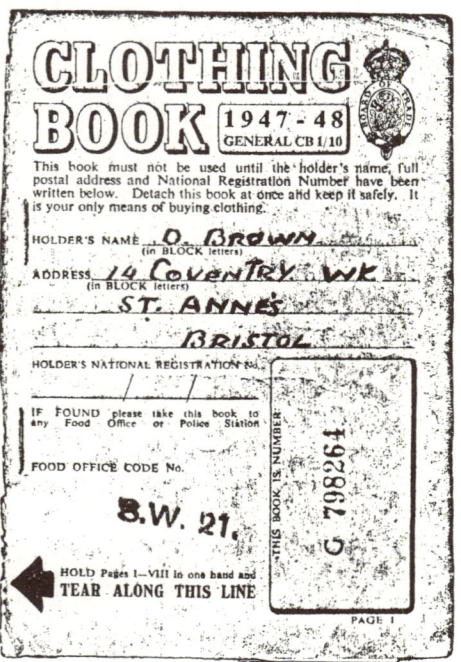

Fig. 22.6 A book of clothing coupons

You see the historian needs to be a 'Sherlock Holmes' on occasions. (I would strongly suggest that if you ever conduct a search like this when doing your project work, you go with an adult who can help you by either finding the places for you, or even asking the questions. It can be very difficult asking questions of total strangers. Remember always to tell people why you are asking the questions.)

The other two examples in this group show **furniture stamps** and **clothing coupons**. These were issued to people in Britain during the War of 1939 to 1945 and for a few years after, when all clothes and furniture and, of course, food were in very short supply and, therefore, shared out fairly by the use of ration cards and stamps such as these. These examples would be useful only for general interest and for illustrating a piece of work. As an historical document it tells us very little about the person they were issued to except the names and address at the time. The fact that they had to be issued, however, does tell us about conditions of life at that time.

22.4 School documents

Another example of a personal document is the school report. Unlike the other examples, school reports were not always issued, and because they are often long forgotten by the person who received them, they take a lot of searching for. They are also the type of thing that some people throw away or lose among the papers and 'junk' that everybody collects. However, if you find them, they can make very interesting reading and can give you some indication of the types of subjects that were taught in schools at a particular time. (Remember that **compulsory** education was not introduced into Britain until 1870 so you will only find school reports before this time if a relative of yours in the past, an **ancestor**, attended an old **public school** such as Eton or Harrow or Rugby.) If you have somebody's school reports, it is possible to trace not only their progress through school, but also to see which subjects they decided to give up, if any, at various stages of their school career.

Not all schools issued termly or half-yearly reports. Some people only received a report or character assessment when they left school, so you may be looking for only one piece of paper.

Examine the school report shown. It is relatively recent. We will see in Volume 2 how we can compare and use school reports to give us an idea of social conditions at the time.

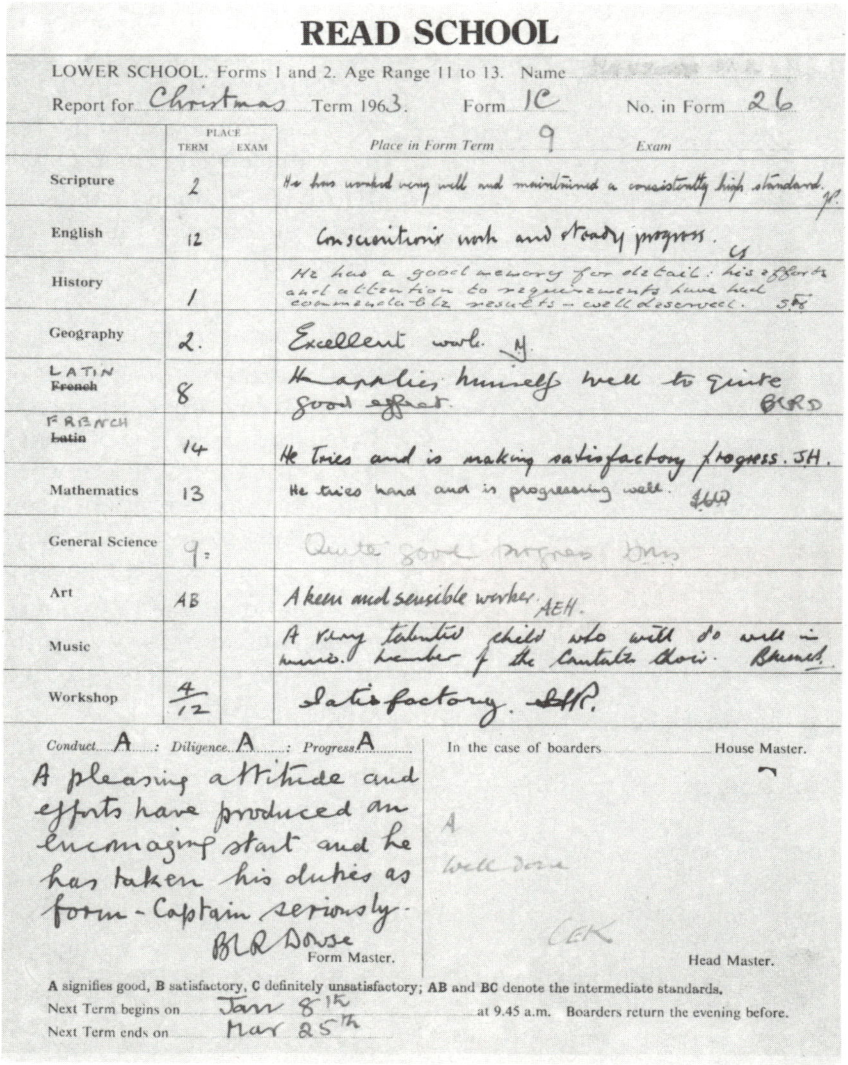

READ SCHOOL

LOWER SCHOOL. Forms 1 and 2. Age Range 11 to 13. Name [illegible]

Report for Christmas Term 1963. Form 1C No. in Form 26

	Place: Term	Place: Exam	Place in Form Term 9 Exam
Scripture	2		He has worked very well and maintained a consistently high standard. JP
English	12		Conscientious work and steady progress. CJ
History	1		He has a good memory for detail: his efforts and attention to requirements have had commendable results – well deserved. SH
Geography	2.		Excellent work. MJ
LATIN ~~French~~	8		He applies himself well to quite good effect. BKRD
FRENCH ~~Latin~~	14		He tries and is making satisfactory progress. JH.
Mathematics	13		He tries hard and is progressing well.
General Science	9.		Quite good progress
Art	AB		A keen and sensible worker. AEH.
Music			A very talented child who will do well in music. Member of the Cantata Choir.
Workshop	4/12		Satisfactory.

Conduct A : Diligence A : Progress A

A pleasing attitude and efforts have produced an encouraging start and he has taken his duties as form-Captain seriously.
BLR Dowse
Form Master.

In the case of boarders .... House Master.

A well done

Head Master.

A signifies good, B satisfactory, C definitely unsatisfactory; AB and BC denote the intermediate standards.
Next Term begins on Jan 8th at 9.45 a.m. Boarders return the evening before.
Next Term ends on Mar 25th

Fig. 22.7

Unit 22 continued

How can this example or similar ones that you may find be useful to you? The report is for Christmas term 1963 and shows that the person concerned studied all the subjects you would expect a first-year pupil to study today. But, are there any subjects here that you do not do at your school today? Do you study Latin in your first year? Which word near the bottom of this report gives us a clue as to the type of school this person attended?

It is possible to trace someone's academic or school career by finding school certificates or CSE, O- and A-level certificates, and either apprenticeship forms or City and Guild certificates or a college or university certificate. All of these will be useful to you when you study your family at a later date. If you find these documents now and cannot keep them, make a note of where to find them again later.

Remember these are only a very few examples of the type of personal documentation you may come across. We will look at ways of using them when we discuss these and other more difficult examples in more detail in Volume 2. It is very important that, as and when you find any material like this, which you think may be useful to you in your studies, you make a note of either all the details you require from the document at the time, or make sure you know where you can find the same document again at a later date. It will save you a lot of time.

Activities

Questions

1 In which year did the Marriage Act become law?
2 What was the rank and profession of the bride's father?
3 What was the name of the person who conducted the service?
4 What position did he hold in this particular church?
5 In which country did this wedding take place?
6 Which entry on the certificate would help you find the original information on the register?
7 In England and Wales there are two types of birth certificate, what are they and what are the differences between them?
8 From which year has it been compulsory for all births, deaths and marriages in England and Wales to be registered?
9 Who is responsible for looking after local registers in England and Wales?
10 Copies of all these certificates since the above date can be found at a particular building in London. Where is it and what is it called?

Summary

1 Marriage, birth and death certificates are all issued on the authority of the Government. They can provide the historian with a great deal of useful information.

2 This information can often provide the historian with a starting point for future study.

3 All births, marriages and deaths in England and Wales since 1 July 1837 should have been registered.

4 Copies of these can be searched for at St Catherine's House in the Aldwych, London.

5 Government documents such as identity cards and clothing coupons issued to individuals give the historian an idea of what life must have been like at the time. In other words they identify the problems which brought about the need for such documents to be issued. They provide little information about the person they were issued to.

6 A national identity card provides all the changes of address of the named person between a number of years. They were issued in 1939 and stopped in 1952.

7 Compulsory education was not introduced into Britain until 1870. Therefore only public school reports are available before that time.

8 If possible, when you come across a document you consider useful, write down all the relevant information you require. If this is not possible make sure you know where to find the same document in the future.

Unit 23

The search for documents and records

In Unit 22 we looked at examples of personal records and documents which you might find in a search of likely places in your home. However, there are still many other types of documents and records which can be extremely useful to the historian, and yet are not personal ones and cannot be found in a search at home. They vary from a simple shopping list from a hundred years ago to a document referring to the business of a large company. Certain examples such as accounts, lists and log-books will be dealt with in more detail in Volume 2, and you will find that you will need to examine many such documents in the project section of Volume 3. But where do you look for these documents if you need them?

23.1 Tracing a document

Usually, after a number of years, most old documents from local companies, or government departments, village council records or school log-books are sent to, and stored in, various government offices, local reference libraries and records' offices. It would be an impossible task to look at all the documents held by such offices on the odd chance of finding one which you think could be helpful to a particular project or topic. Not only would it be very time consuming and boring, but it would provide you with very few worthwhile results for the amount of time you spent in the search. Therefore, you need a method which will cut down the 'searching' time. There are two ways of going about such an investigation.

The starting point

Let us imagine that you wish to find the log-book of a primary school in your area for the year 1875. The first thing you need to do is find out where all the local records for this period of history are kept. Most probably they will be stored at your nearest county records' office, which is usually in the main county town or in the town where the county council has its offices. (You can find out this information from your local library or by looking up county council offices in your telephone directory.)

Make an appointment

Having tracked them down to your county records' office you now need to search for the documents you require. But, before you start, it is always best to ring the records' office first so that they have some idea of what you are looking for and also so that they can reserve a desk for you in case they have a lot of 'researchers' at the same time. Also, if you know what you are looking for, they will usually be able to tell you over the telephone whether or not they have an example of it. If they have not, the call will certainly save you a wasted journey, but they may even be able to suggest another document which would suit your purpose. It will also give the **archivists** a chance to check with their colleagues whether or not the documents you require are available or suitable for you to see.

At the records office

We will assume that the log-book you require is available. When you arrive at the records' office you will be certain to see a reception desk; always go there first, tell them who you are and that you rang them previously, and remind them of the document you wish to see. They will probably ask you to sign a visitors' book so that they know who used the offices on that particular day. If it is the first time you have been to the office a member of the archivist staff will show you around and explain the type of documents available to you. If the archivist does not have the time to find your document for you, how do you go about it? We will use the same example of a school log-book and try to find the one for the village school in Crookham for the year 1875. Crookham is in Berkshire so you would have to go to the records' office in the Shire Hall in Reading, the county town.

Filing systems

In the office you will find a set of files, usually small boxes containing cards about the size of a postcard. These boxes will contain two different indexes referring to the material available. One set of files will be the parish index listing all the parishes in the county and the information available from the parish kept in the office. This will be indexed alphabetically. (See page 75.) The other set will contain an index of subjects, for example, accounts, estate records, education. You now have two ways of finding the location of your document.

First look up the village of Crookham in the parish index. If the parish does not appear on the file, you will need to find out which parish Crookham is in, in this case I will tell you that it is in Thatcham. Therefore, look up the card for

Unit 23 continued

THATCHAM	School Records	
1864–1964	Log-books of Thatcham Church of England School.	C/EL 53/1,2–6*
1875–1957	Log-book of Crookham School.	C/EL 36/1–3*
1794–1860	Minutes and accounts of Lady Frances Winchcombe's Charity School.	D/P 130/25/6
1913–1955	School Managers' minutes.	C/EM 19,67*
1900–1957	Crookham C. of E. (Controlled) School.	C/EZ 7*
1945–1946	Registers of British School, S., JM and I. departments.	C/ER 32*

* restricted

Fig. 23.1

C/EL/	Berkshire Record Office: Education – School Log-Books 3		
29	Burghfield Common (Mrs Bland's).	1 vol.	1873–1905
30/1,2	Didcot, The Manor School, Church of England.	2 vols.	1881–1903
31	Didcot, Board (Evening School).	1 vol.	1896–1904
32	Didcot, Board (Infant's class).	1 vol.	1887–1918
33	Woolhampton, Church of England.		
34/1,2	Maidenhead, Boyne Hill Infant's.	2 vols.	1866–1905
35/1,2	East Hagbourne Church of England.	2 vols.	1875–1954
36/1–3	Crookham (parish of Thatcham).	3 vols.	1875–1957
37	Little Coxwell Church of England.	1 vol.	1888–1916

Fig. 23.2

the parish of Thatcham. On the cards there will be either a short description of the available documents for Thatcham or simply a reference number. In this case there is a card marked 'school records' and the reference number for the log-book of Crookham school, as you can see in the example, is C/EL 36/1–3. (Fig. 23.1).

Types of index

If you find that your records' office does not have a subject index and the parish index only provides you with the reference numbers and no descriptions, you would have to look up all the references on the card until you found the document you needed. If, however, there is a subject index, you need to find the card for school records or education. On the file card you should see a number identical to the one on the Thatcham Parish Card i.e. C/EL 36/1–3. This document is therefore the one you require (Fig. 23.2).

Once you have found the reference number you simply pick up a **document requisition form** from the reception desk, (Fig. 23.3) and hand it in at the desk. They will then find the document for you and bring it to your desk where you can use it (Fig. 23.4).

Fig. 23.3

BERKSHIRE RECORD OFFICE

Document Required (Catalogue Mark)	Reader's Name (Block Capitals)	
Date Required	For conditions see over	
FOR OFFICE USE ONLY		
Produced by	Replaced by	Storage
Date	Date	No. of documents

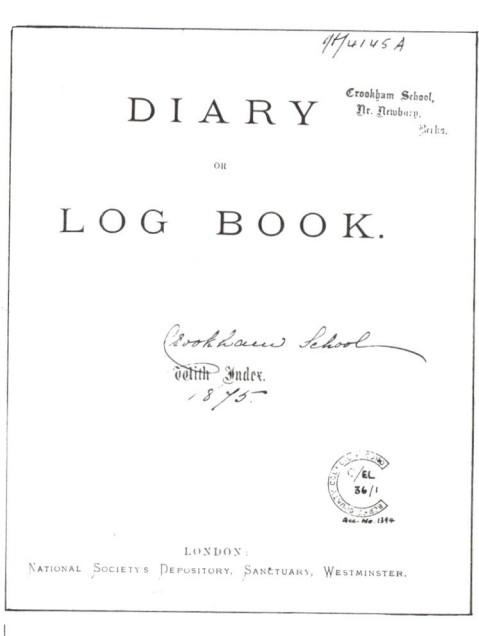

Fig. 23.4 Log book cover and inside page

23.2 Handling a document

You will be allowed to use only pencil in the records' office so remember to take one with you. However, if you forget you will usually find some on sale at the desk. If you wish to trace a map you will not be allowed to trace straight from it; ask at the desk for a piece of clear plastic or perspex which you can lay on top of the map, and then place the tracing paper on top of this and trace as usual.

Remember there are other people in the office who are doing research as well as yourself, so always walk and never run, and if you have to, always speak in a whisper, so as not to disturb your neighbour.

Activities

Alphabetical indexes are very easy to follow if all the references you are looking for begin with A,B,C etc. However, it becomes a little more difficult if you have two or more references beginning with the same letter e.g. Aldermaston and Arborfield. Where do these come in an alphabetical order since they both begin with A? In this case you look at the **second** letter of each word, and because **Al** comes before **Ar** Aldermaston would appear in the file before Arborfield. If the second letters are the same you would look at the **third** and so on until there is a difference. For example, Aldershot and Aldermaston:— Alder**m** comes before Alder**s** so Aldermaston would appear on the file first.

Sort out the following list into alphabetical order:

Falkirk	Kingswood	Alnmouth
Bishop Auckland	Portsmouth	Bexhill
Hampton	Wallingford	Aldworth
Yattendon	Enfield	Newmarket
Zetland	Milford	Oxford
Falkland	Kingston	Ashford
Bishop Castle	Saltash	

Summary

1 Ring your local records' office to ask if they have the document or an equivalent example you may use. Reserve a desk.

2 On arrival report to the reception desk and say who you are.

3 *Either* look up the village that interests you in the parish index. Find the description and/or the reference number of the document you require. Fill in a requisition form, hand it in at the desk and wait.

or look up the subject of the document in the subject index and find a reference to your particular study area. Look at the reference number, fill in a requisition form, hand it in at the desk and wait.

4 In our example the reference for Crookham school C/EL/36 1–3 appears on both cards (Figs. 23.1 and 23.2).

Unit 24

Place names

In Units 22 and 23 we looked generally at the type of document which you would probably find useful when studying your family history. In Unit 23 we looked at ways of finding documents at your local records' office and extracting information about your local area. But often a clue to the origins of the area you are interested in can sometimes be found very easily. For example, have you ever wondered how your town or village got its name. Finding its **original** name, and remember it may have changed its spelling over the years (e.g. **Bricgstow** = **Bristol**, the place on the bridge), will give you a rough idea of how old your settlement could be; there are clues in the way the name is spelt which can provide the historian with a starting point in his investigation. But how and why were these names given, and what clues do you need to look out for?

24.1 Original population – the Celts

During the early period of British history, just before and after the birth of Christ, the country was invaded by a series of conquering groups from foreign countries in search of tin, gold, land and even wives! The original British people, those living in the country before these invasions took place, were called **Celts**. They spoke Celtic so their settlements were given Celtic names. However, as each succeeding foreign group came into Britain these Celts were pushed westwards into the mountains of Wales, where they established the Welsh language, south-west into the moorlands of Cornwall, where they spoke Cornish, and North into the highlands of Scotland where they spoke Gaelic. As they moved they established new settlements and, unless you are used to reading or understanding Welsh, Gaelic or other Celtic-based languages you will probably find a lot of the names difficult to pronounce.

24.2 The invaders

1. The Romans

There are many examples of Celtic-named settlements in these three areas of the country, for example, Llanberis and Llandovery in Wales,

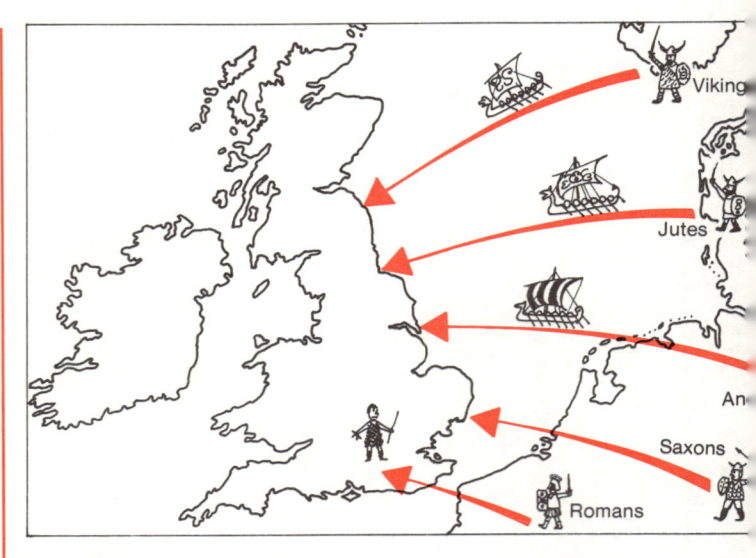

Fig. 24.1 Map showing various invasions of Britain throughout history

Penzance and Marazion in Cornwall and places such as Thurso and Tighnabruaich in Scotland. The first invading group to push the Celts out of the southern area of Britain was **the Romans**. They originally came from the city of Rome in Italy, and before they came to Britain, they had conquered most of Europe, including Gaul, (modern France) from where they launched their invasion of Britain.

The Romans were a **military power** and because the invading force was, of course, an army, their first settlements were mainly fortified army camps. These camps were surrounded with wooden walls to protect them from attacks by the Celts. Some of these villages remained for a time as armed camps, some were eventually abandoned altogether, and over the years, especially in peace time, some of the building development took place outside the original walls.

Latin was the Roman language and the Latin word for **fortified camp** was **caster** or **castra**. Therefore, many early Roman settlements have names ending with the letters caster, cester, or chester. Examples of such Roman towns are numerous, for example, Chester, Silchester and Colchester.

2. The Saxons

When the next conquering group, the Saxons, came to Britain from Europe they were less concerned about fighting and more concerned about farming. Therefore, many of the name endings of some of the settlements they established have something to do with farming. A village name ending with the letters **tun, ton, on, wick, wich** or **ham** suggests that the original settlement had something to do with an actual farm, for example, Kingston = King's ton = the farm belonging to the king. Shepton would originally have been Sheepton = Sheep ton = Sheep farm. Alnwick = Aln (a river in Northumberland) Wick = the farm near the River Aln.

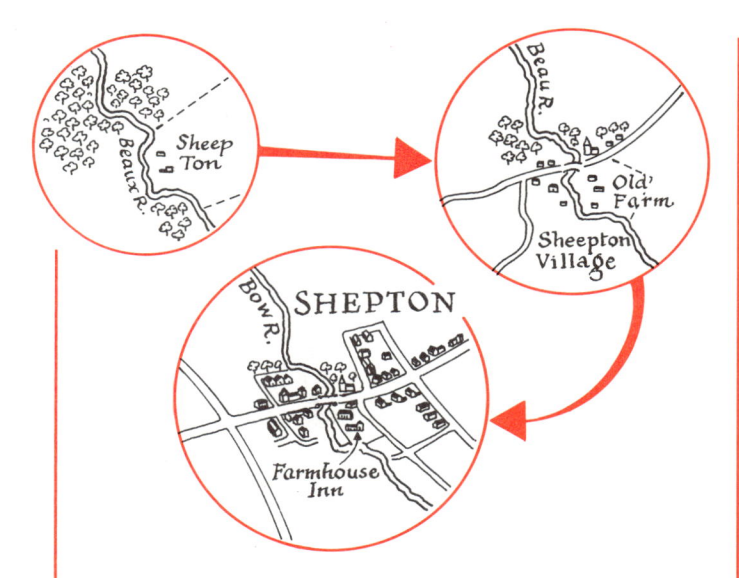

Names ending with the letters **ley** or **leigh** the Saxon word for **clearing** suggests that somewhere near the original settlement was a clearing used for some purpose, for example, Cowley = cow ley = a clearing used for cow pasture. Northleigh = north leigh = north clearing.

The Saxon ending **burgh** means a **fort** so Edinburgh = Edwin's burgh = Edwin's fortified place.

The letters **hamm** meant **meadow** or enclosure or water meadow. This is not to be confused with the Saxon **ham** which also meant **farm**. However, the second *m* may have been left off a document at some time in the past, so you see it is very important to find the earliest possible spelling of the village name in order to be as accurate as possible.

3. The Vikings

When the Vikings or Danes sailed across the North Sea from **Scandinavia** to attack, conquer and eventually settle in areas in the north and east of England, they left evidence of their movement across the country by the distinctive endings to the names they gave their villages. The letters **thorpe** meant a **hamlet**, or small village. So a settlement called West Thorpe would simply mean west hamlet. (Presumably there must have been other hamlets in the area so this one must have been the most westerly one and so named to distinguish it from the others.) The letters **by** meant **homestead** and the ending **borough** meant a **fort**. So for example Middlesbrough would mean middle fort, again there must have been others of which this was the middle one.

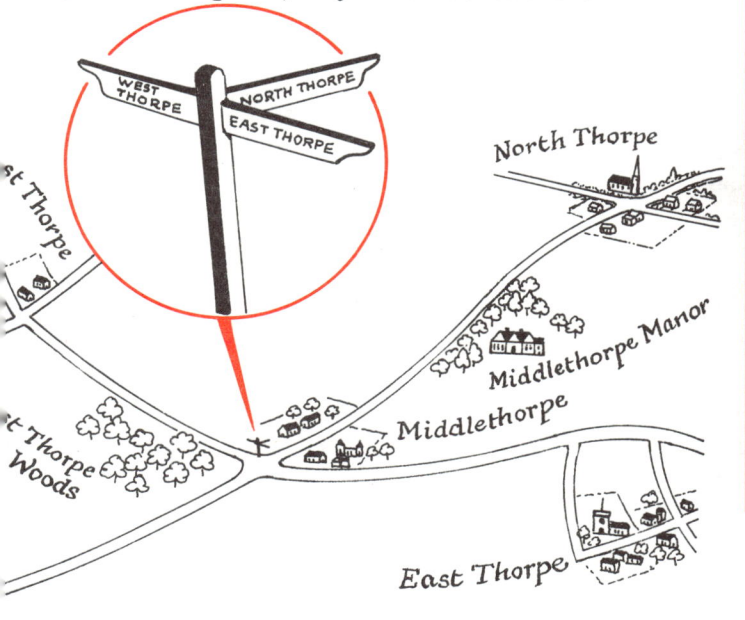

24.3 Further study

Not only are the name endings of these various groups interesting, from the point of view of finding out the origins of your particular village, but it is possible, by looking at a large-scale map with all the small settlements marked on it, to trace the complete area settled by one of these invaders. We could, for instance, find out how far the Vikings travelled inland from the coast, or how far the Saxons moved west after they had settled in the south-east. This type of investigation is far too complicated for you to undertake at present, but it does suggest what is possible.

24.4 Names according to occupation

Each invading group which spread across Britain in her early history left evidence of the settlements they established by the names they gave them. However, not all places were named in this way. Some of them were simply given a name which suggested the type of work or occupation which was going on, either in the village itself, or in the surrounding area. Usually most of the endings had something to do with farming, or the land because until the late 1700s most people had jobs concerned in some way with the land.

There was no industry in the same way as today. Such name endings include **field**, or **wood** e.g. Bradfield = broadfield meaning a large area

Unit 24 continued

of land. Kingswood = king's wood, the wood belonging to the king. Some names referred to the most important building in the area, for instance Abbeytown, the town near the abbey. Other names refer to specific things, for example, before the introduction of bridges across rivers, the only way to get from one side to the other was by walking or wading across at a shallow point on the river – a **ford**. Therefore the name ford told the people that at that spot there was a way across the water, e.g. Oxford. Later more bridges were built, so many settlements have the ending **bridge** e.g. Cambridge the bridge over the river Cam, or Newbridge simply a new bridge. Some names suggest a geographical site, for example, the mouth of a river: Teignmouth – the settlement at the mouth of the river Teign in Devon, or Alnmouth a coastal village at the mouth of the river Aln in Northumberland.

Fig. 24.2 What does this city sign tell you?

Look carefully at the name

Some names are not what they first seem. For instance the village of Redgrave is not as you would expect, the site of a red grave, but in fact it refers to a reed grove. These reeds were especially grown for use by thatchers.

Others seem funny today, but on closer inspection can be useful. The village name of Piddletrenthide in Dorset can be divided into three distinct parts to provide us with its original meaning: piddle = puddle = marsh; trent = thirty; hide = an area of land of approximately 120 acres in size. Therefore, this name simply means an area of marshy land covering an area of thirty hides.

24.5 Names according to owner

The meaning of some names which were given to places in the past suggest that they were either owned by a particular person or perhaps they were used as a popular local meeting place, so popular in fact that people eventually settled near it. For example in the 7th and 8th centuries an **alderman** was referred to as 'A Nobleman of the highest rank beneath the king or queen'. Therefore the village of Aldermaston simply refers to the Alderman's farm or estate. Later, in the 10th century, the name **earl** replaced alderman so some of the settlements and estates were called earlston(e) = Earl's Farm, or Arleston meaning the same thing.

24.6 Names according to meeting places

Meeting places often gave their names to the settlement surrounding them and were usually named after the tree under which the meeting gathered, for example Matlock = the oak beneath which the meeting was held, and Matlask = the ash beneath which the meeting is held. Runnymede where King John met his barons in June 1215 to discuss and sign the Magna Carta, was a well-known meeting place of the time. It means meadow at a runy, runy meaning 'an island where a council is held'.

24.7 Look carefully at the name

There are many common name endings in Britain, too many to mention here. Some of them are given to very recent settlements so you occasionally find a new village with an old name ending. Even a town two or three hundred years old may have been given a name which looks as if it is of Saxon or Danish origin. So before you take it for granted that your village or town name means that it was once a Viking fort or a Saxon farm, it is worth checking the name in another source of information.

It is most important to remember that the modern spelling of a town or village name can be very different from the original. As we saw with the two Saxon endings **ham** and **hamm**, which have different meanings, it would have been very easy for someone writing about this second settlement to have left off the second 'm' so changing the original meaning of the name. Therefore, remember that it is necessary to find the earliest possible spelling of the name in order to be accurate.

Where to look

The best place to look for this original spelling would be in a local library or local records' office, or in a book which gives you information about the towns and villages in your particular county or area. These often give, not only the original and up-to-date spelling, but also the changes in between. For example, the town of Reading in Berkshire, (meaning the persons and goods belonging to a man called Red or Read), has been written at various stages in history as Reding, Reddinge and Redding and many others. (It is interesting to note that a part of Reading has changed its spelling and yet seems to have kept its original meaning: Erlegh has become Early; it may be simply that someone forgot the original spelling or perhaps some writer in the past was just a little lazy.)

Activities

1 (a) Using the clues available in Unit 24 divide the following list of places into Celtic, Roman, Saxon, Danish/Viking and others (those that refer to a building or geographical feature).

(b) When you have listed them, explain the possible original meaning of those marked*.

ABBEY TOWN, CASTLETON*, BAMBURGH, DALTON, BRIDGENORTH*, RAYLEIGH, LEICESTER, AVONMOUTH*, SHEPTON*, RAMPTON*, PORTLAND, ATTLEBOROUGH*, BILSTON, BARHAM*, KENTFORD*, CAMELFORD*, DORCHESTER, BINGLEY, ASHFORDBY, SANDWICK, STOCKBRIDGE*, HATFIELD, YSTRAD, ALTHORPE, NORTHWICH*, SCARBOROUGH, EDINBURGH*, NEWTON*, WATLINGTON, TREFNANT, NEWBURGH, RINGWOOD

2 What else does the name Middlesbrough suggest to the historian apart from the meaning of the name?

3 Apart from the spelling, what is the difference in origin between Edinburgh and Scarborough?

4 Using one of the examples from the list, design a town badge showing the origins of the name, for example, Shepton could be shown as a sheep in a pen or in a field, or simply a sheep on a green background.

5 Search your local area and try to work out the possible origins of some of the settlements.

Summary

1 The original inhabitants of Britain, the Celts, were forced to move west and north as each new invasion took place.

2 The Romans were a military power and their original settlements were mainly armed camps.

3 The Saxons were farmers and most of the name endings of their settlements have something to do with farming the land.

4 The Vikings sailed from Scandinavia and originally settled on the north and east coast of England.

5 Celtic names: are in Welsh, Cornish and Gaelic and are often difficult to pronounce.

Roman names: often end in caster, cester or chester.

Saxon names: -tun, -ton, -on, -wick, -wich, -ham = farm; hamm = meadow or enclosure; -ley, -leigh = clearing or pasture; burgh = fortified place.

Viking names: by = homestead; thorpe = hamlet; borough = fort.

6 Some village names have something to do with the surrounding area and were not necessarily given by an invading group.

7 Some names refer to important people or places in the area.

8 It is very important when looking at place names to find the earliest spelling possible in order accurately to work out its meaning.

9 Information about a local name can be found in a local library, the records' office or a book dealing with places in your particular county.

Unit 25

Introduction to building styles

In Unit 24 you were given enough simple clues to help you work out the possible origins of your town or village. The development of that settlement is, of course, a very important part of its history, and clues to this growth can be seen in the objects that you see around you every day and take for granted – the buildings.

Let us look at the way in which building materials and styles have changed over the years.

25.1 Influence of building materials available

Wood

It is almost certain that the majority of houses in your settlement are built out of brick and stone. However, this was not the case before the 1600s. The most popular building material for houses before the 17th century was wood. A lot of the country, especially the river valleys, was thickly covered with oak forests, so wood was easily available. Oak was used in the building construction and elm was used for anything to do with water, pipes, weather protection etc. The problem to the historian is that wood rots and decays over a period of time, so few of these houses still survive today in their original form. Some have been strengthened and some have had new walls built in brick or stone to stop them falling down, but few are the same as when they were first built.

Stone

Before the 1600s stone was usually only used for the most important buildings, and the most important building in any village community (there were few towns) was **the church**. The church was always built in stone and great care was given to it. It was the centre of village life until the middle 1500s, and all the skilled men in the area, the stonemasons, carpenters etc, were called in to do their best jobs. Because the churches were stone, and because stone does not rot away like wood, most of them have survived to the present day. Therefore, it is usual for the church to be the oldest building in the village.

Sometimes you may find **a castle** very close to your particular settlement. They were also built in stone, and like houses, changed in style and patterns over hundreds of years. They housed the lords and barons and their families, and were also used as a base for the soldiers when keeping the local population in check. By the end of the 15th century however, castle building had stopped. The invention and introduction of gunpowder meant they could now be destroyed by cannon-balls, so it was not worth going to the expense of building any new ones.

Fig. 25.1 The castle, Richmond, North Yorkshire

Brick

By the 17th and 18th centuries timber was becoming very scarce, and bricks were becoming cheaper, so there was a complete change in building styles. All new buildings were now built out of brick and stone, and by the 18th century large areas of towns owned by the same landlord could be built to this owner's own design. That is why you can see large open squares with houses around them in London, and long crescent-shaped streets in Bath.

Fig. 25.2 Royal Crescent, Bath

25.2 Influence of social conditions

Often many settlements grew up around the walls of the castle. The ordinary people relied on it for their livelihood, either growing crops or raising food to be sold to the castle kitchens, or working as servants or grooms. The houses were wooden and few have survived, so we can only guess what they looked like from old pictures; but we do know that, because of the lack of space around the castle walls, they were all huddled together and very unhygienic; disease was very common and a fire in one of them would easily destroy many others. Sometimes these villages actually grew up within the walls of the castle and some developed around a church or cathedral.

Growth of trade

By the 1400s the population in Britain was growing very fast and there was a great increase in trade and wealth. The historian sees the beginnings of small towns and cities developing because of this trade. Most of the buildings were still wooden, but the new wealthy traders now built themselves new manor-houses or farm-houses out of brick and stone. Most of this stone came from the local area because it was impossible, until the building of the canals and railways in the late 1700s and early 1800s, to move stone from one area of the country to another cheaply.

Homes for the wealthy

During the 1500s or Tudor times, many of the wealthy people required comfortable houses and most of these were built either in brick or brick with oak beams. The ordinary people still lived in wooden houses which were usually plastered with reeds and limestone.

The Industrial Revolution

The biggest change in housing came about because of the Industrial Revolution, and if you live in the Midlands or the North of Britain, you are certain to find evidence of the then new **iron and steel industries**. There was a great change from people working on farms and estates to working in the mills and factories. Because they needed to live near their work, rows and rows of cheap houses were built, often by the factory owners themselves, and rented by the workers.

Iron became very fashionable and not only was it used to build and decorate houses, but, because it had to be moved around the countryside, **new railway stations**, iron bridges and iron viaducts were built to carry the new transport system. Railways also meant that people no longer had to live close to their place of work. They could now commute, or travel daily by train. **Suburbs** grew up around the edges of towns and cities. Many of the small village stations were closed in the 1960s, but it is possible to see them now used for totally different purposes. Some railway sheds have become small warehouses and some stations have become private houses.

Building styles were changed and influenced by the social conditions of the time and the building materials available, and it is these styles and changes which provide the historian with the clues needed to trace the development of an individual building or village. In Units 26, 27 and 28 we will see what these clues are.

Summary

1 The most important buildings in an area were almost always built in stone. The church is, therefore, often the oldest building in a settlement, because the wooden buildings would have rotted and decayed.

2 Trade and wealth in the 13th and 14th century led to the beginnings of small towns and cities based on this trade.

3 After the 17th century, timber became very scarce and bricks became common.

4 Before the introduction of canals and railways, all building material came from the local area. Therefore, different areas of the country have different styles of buildings and different building materials.

5 No castles were built in the old style after the 1500s because the introduction of gunpowder meant that they could be easily destroyed.

Unit 26

Building styles up to 1500s

26.1 Clues to the age of a building

Having looked at the reasons why building styles may have changed over the years we now need to look at clues available which may help you decide upon the approximate age of a particular building.

Plaques

The simplest clues often appear on the house itself. Sometimes the date of the building is written on a plaque set into the wall (Fig. 26.1), or written in a brick pattern across a number of houses. Sometimes the name of a row of houses may be seen and occasionally this is the name of the builder who built them.

Fig. 26.1

Records' offices

If you know the area you wish to study, it is again worth going to your local library or records' office. The librarian, or books on your particular county may give you the approximate date or age of the town or village you are interested in and will give you a starting point from which to continue your studies. It will also help you decide whether a building in this area is genuine or not. For example, if you find that your village was not established until 1850 you will not see any genuine Tudor-built houses, so if there are any of this style, they are copies.

The church

Another area where you could find help in working out the possible date from which the settlement developed is the church. We have already said that most of the old wooden houses made from the oak and elm have rotted away, therefore the church, built of stone, is likely to be the oldest surviving building in the village. If it does not have a pamphlet on sale explaining its origins, you can work out its likely age in two ways: *either* by finding a list of vicars or rectors, usually found on the wall inside the church (the first appointment e.g. Rev A.N. Other 1297 will

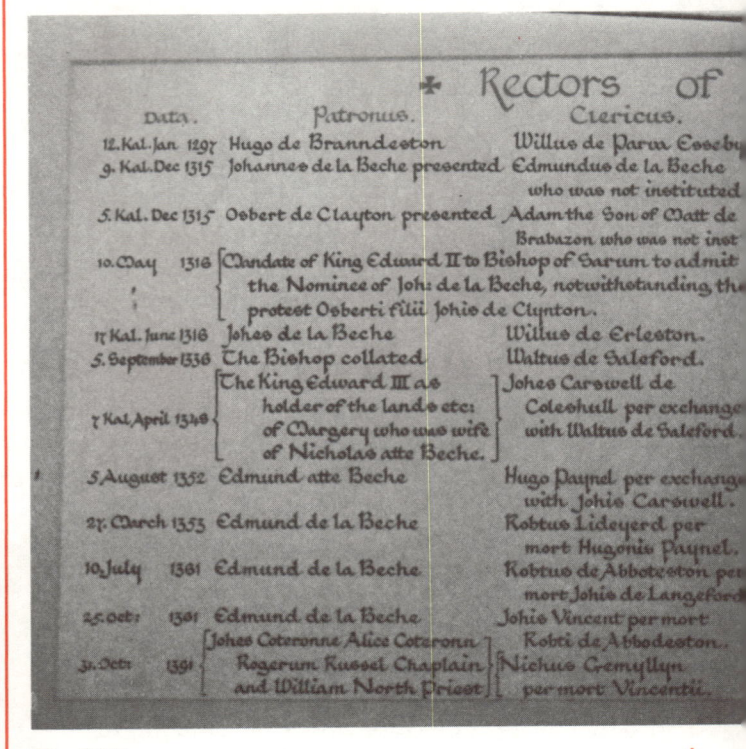

Fig. 26.2

tell you that there was a church and, therefore, a congregation and, therefore, a village to house them in 1297), *or* by finding the oldest gravestone in the churchyard. This is less accurate because many of the early gravemarkers were made from wood and they too have gradually rotted away and have not been replaced. (We will look more closely at the importance of the church in the project section of Volume 3.)

26.2 Features of a pre-Tudor building

Stone buildings

Although we said that most of the original wooden buildings in an area have disappeared, it is still possible to find very old houses, built from local stone in areas where timber was scarce. It is still possible to find very old examples of houses built from local granite in Cornwall.

The cottages were usually **'squat'** and very small and would have either stone tiles or thatch on the roofs. The doorways and windows would have been small to cut down on draughts and originally the windows would have been covered with wooden shutters rather than glass.

Fig. 26.3 A fine example of Tudor cottages

Wooden buildings

Those timber-framed houses which do survive have their own clues which will help you date them. Some of the features are, in fact, caused by their age. The original **foundations** of these buildings were often shallow and many of the survivors seem to sag or bend over at the top. If you find a number of these houses together and look at the roof-ridge, you will see that it is very uneven. The doors were smaller than today's and the window panes were very small.

Glass was very expensive, so if people could not afford it they used wooden shutters, or in the case of even poorer people, cloth to cover the window hole in the wall. This meant that again the houses were dark inside and very cold in the winter.

Oak beams

The most common recognizable feature of a Tudor house is the large oak beams which can be seen on the outside (Fig. 26.3). Usually the floor beams holding up the upper floor came through to the front of the house and can actually be seen on the exterior. The upper storeys of Tudor houses often hung over the storey beneath and it was possible for some houses on either side of a Tudor street almost to touch the one opposite at the top. The Tudor style has often been copied by designers, especially in the 1930s and in the 1980s, but a close look at the beams should tell you whether or not the house is genuinely Tudor.

Summary

Pre-Tudor, before 1500

1. There are few surviving wooden buildings because the wood rotted away.
2. In areas where trees were in short supply, and stone was plentiful, the early houses were made from the local stone.
3. These houses were very small and squat with roofs covered in split-stone or thatch.

Tudor

1. Poor foundations, therefore, the surviving buildings seem to sag.
2. Roof-line usually uneven.
3. Succeeding storeys overhang the ones below.
4. Doors small. (It is known that on average people were shorter in the Tudor period than they are today.)
5. Irregular-shaped small windows with small panes of glass.
6. Windows opened outwards.
7. Beams supporting the upper storeys often came through to the front of the house.

Unit 27

Building styles 1700 to 1910

Since the time that early man had built a simple wooden shelter from the materials around him the most common building material, except in areas where there were few trees, had been timber. However, by the mid-1700s supplies of timber had gradually declined. At the same time, however, the making of bricks had improved and they were now easily available. Therefore, this brought about a change in house-building.

27.1 Georgian: 1700 to 1820

Fewer new houses from this time onwards were built from wood and it was usually only used for doors and window-frames. The new houses in this Georgian period were taller than the previous styles and were very popular in pattern. Some were **symmetrical** i.e. if you take a line down through the centre of the house the left-hand side would be identical to the right. The windows were much larger than before. They were rectangular, with small rectangular panes of glass, and, unlike the side opening windows of Tudor houses, these opened 'up and down' and were moved by **sashes** inside the window-frames.

Apart from the style of window the other significant clue to the houses of this period is the position of a **fanlight** above the front door. This was usually in the shape of half an orange with the segments of glass going out from the centre (see Fig. 27.2). Some larger and more ornate Georgian houses had a row of small capped pillars going across the front of the house just below the roof-line, this feature is called a **balustrade**. It is also from this period that the large squares in London and the crescent-shaped streets of Bath were established.

Fig. 27.2 A Georgian fanlight

Fig. 27.1 A Georgian house

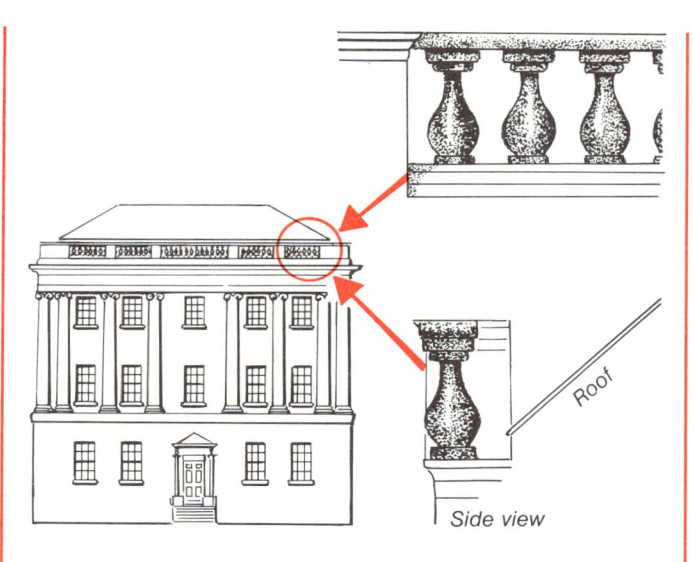

Fig. 27.3 A balustrade

Social conditions

Remember that the styles of building described above could only be afforded by the wealthy, so in a village you would probably only find them as the old manor-house or, perhaps, the vicarage or rectory where the vicar, at the time a very important man in the life of the village, lived. The ordinary person's living conditions were not very good. They often lived in village houses that had not changed for two or three hundred years.

27.2 Victorian: 1820 to 1910

By the end of the 18th century, Britain was well into the Industrial Revolution and because of the movement from village to town, and from the farms to the factories, many town houses and workers' cottages had to be built quickly, and often very badly. These usually had two rooms upstairs and two rooms downstairs with an earth 'privy' at the bottom of the garden, if there was one. Alternatively there was a privy at the end of a row of houses where it was shared by all the other households.

Bricks were cheap so all the buildings were brick built and the roofs were covered in thin black slates. The windows were smaller in size than the Georgian ones and they opened outwards. Some of the houses designed for the slightly better-off in the late 1880s often had bay windows and larger rooms. The outsides were also decorated by using one or two different colours of bricks in different patterns. An example of one of these patterns informs the historian of the actual date the house or row of houses was built (see Fig. 27.4). There were few **terraced** houses of this kind in villages, but the same features can be seen in any new building of the period.

Fig. 27.4 In which year were these Victorian houses built?

Unit 27 continued

School buildings

One important village building comes from this time: the village school. Through the Education Act of 1870, education was recognized as a public service in Britain, so there was a rush to build schools, which were controlled by a group of local people or the School Board. These 'Board' schools were very common and are still used in towns and villages today. Some of them now have new extensions, but often the old building is still in full use.

Sometimes the entrances to these schools have the words Boys or Girls or Infants above them because children had to go through the separate doors to the classes and they played in separate playgrounds. Sometimes you can still see the belltower where the school bell hung. Occasionally in a village, the teacher's house was built at the same time and in some cases was actually attached to the school. All Board school windows were a long way from the ground so that the children could not look out of them and so not be distracted from their studies.

Public rooms

As well as the school, many village-halls were also built in order to have somewhere for the whole village to gather for various functions. You may also find a **reading-room** dating from this time. These were usually set up by a wealthy member of the community or the local landowner and often contained a small library and a copy of various newspapers. These rooms were used, before the introduction of public libraries, by members of the village who could not afford to buy books or newspapers. All these examples were built in the same Victorian style. One important clue to Victorian buildings is that they often had a decorated roof-line made from tiles standing on their sides along the ridge of the roof.

Fig. 27.5 See how brickwork achieves an ornate effect on this decorated roof-line.

Fig. 27.6 A separate entrance for infants . . .

Fig. 27.7 . . . and for boys

Summary

Georgian 1700 to 1820

1 Built from brick and stone. In London the white Portland stone was becoming popular.
2 Buildings were taller than before, and the pattern of the front of the house was regular.
3 Large rectangular windows with small rectangular panes. Opened by the use of sash cords.
4 Front doors often have fanlights over the top.
5 Many large country houses built during this period. Larger ones sometimes had a balustrade running along the top just beneath the roof-line.
6 Shop fronts often had bow windows with small panes of glass.

Victorian/Edwardian 1820 to 1910

1 Brick-built, except in areas where stone was common.
2 Works' houses and '2-up, 2-down' styles built in towns and cities during the Industrial Revolution.
3 Many schools, especially village primary schools, date from 1870.
4 Many village halls and reading-rooms also date from this period.
5 Some later houses built for the better off working-class families from 1880 to 1920 had bay-windows and decorated brickwork.
6 Many public buildings in both villages and towns had decorated roof-lines.

Unit 28

Building styles, 20th century

At the beginning of the 20th century Britain was generally a wealthy country and its population was growing fast. Therefore, the development of building styles increased quickly. At the turn of the century there had been a move towards 'garden estates', 'garden cities' and 'garden suburbs', and an attempt was made to clear away many of the Victorian slums from the cities. (This has still to be done in some areas of the country and examples may still be found in some city centres.) Some 19th-century employers laid out new housing estates with gardens for their workers or set aside areas of open space for allotments, and grew wide grass verges along the edges of the roads. Examples of these are the towns of Bourneville near Birmingham and Welwyn Garden City.

28.1 Features 1920 to 1940

The houses built between the years 1920 and 1940 were again built out of brick and they were sometimes decorated with **pebbledash** where cement was put onto the outside wall and small stones and pebbles were thrown onto it. The windows of this period were usually side-opening. Many houses in the new suburbs built around the

Fig. 28.1 An aerial view of Welwyn Garden City

towns and cities had **porches** around their front doors. These were often covered in at a later date with an extra front door to cut down on the draughts and help keep the house warmer, so do not be put off if you see a house which you think is from this time, but which does not seem to have a porch. Many of the front doors had glass in the top half of them. These were often patterned using **coloured glass** and were often in the shape of a rising sun.

Social factors

It is from this time that the first **council house estates** were built. They were usually built on the edge of the towns and cities, but were sometimes constructed in villages around the towns to ease congestion and overcrowding in the centre.

With the increased use of steel, concrete and electricity, which gave **cheap lighting** as well as allowing for the use of **lifts**, the developers were able to build taller and lighter buildings, and because the craftsman's time was now expensive and machines were becoming more efficient, more factory house-building materials were now being used. Therefore, you may find examples in your area of buildings which look as though they have been covered in concrete slabs or which seem to have no bricks in them at all. A lot of houses were built in the 1930s, especially in the wealthier south and midland regions of England, so you are certain to find many examples of dwellings from this period.

Fig. 28.2 (*top*) An example of terraced council houses
Fig. 28.3 (*bottom*) Flats on a council estate

Unit 28 continued

28.2 Features, 1940 to present day

During World War Two, 1939 to 1945, many towns and cities were bombed, and so a lot of housing was lost. This had to be replaced quickly after 1945 so you will find that a lot of buildings from this time have a lot of glass in them. In order to save space, especially in the centres of towns and cities, many **high-rise** flats were built, sometimes ten or fifteen storeys high!

Social factors

With the arrival of the motor car at a price more people could afford, some of the new houses from the mid-1930s onwards had garages, either immediately alongside the house, if space allowed, or in a small group a little distance away. Many from the 1970s and 80s actually have the garage as part of the house itself, often with a room above it.

Modern houses in villages are often found in small groups where there is room, or on their own on a small plot of land between other houses. This type of housing development is called **infilling** and is now very common, especially in the south of England. These are built of brick and have large **picture** windows and, because of the lack of spare land, usually have only small gardens. If they have oil-fired, electric or gas heating they will not have a chimney, so you will be lucky to find one on a modern estate. Although there are few flats to be found in villages, there are often one or two maisonettes, which are the same as flats, but only two storeys high. There is also the practice, in some areas, of building single-bedroomed houses in order to give single people and newly married couples the opportunity of buying a house they can afford.

Clues from shop buildings

Many old buildings in town centres are now shops. If you wish to date buildings in an area where there are shops, do not look at the shop front itself, but just above it. Shop fronts change with fashion from the bow-fronted windows of the Georgian period that you often see on old Christmas cards to the large picture windows of today. The actual building, however, may not change at all. The best way, therefore, of dating such a shop is to look at the roof-line and the shape of the windows on the second storey and see if they correspond to any of the clues you have been given here. If possible look at the back of the shop, easily done if it is on a corner of a street, where it has probably not been changed since it was first built.

Activities

These activities cover Units 25 to 28.

On a poster-size piece of paper, draw six equal columns and give them the following headings: **Age; Building material; Roof material; Windows; Distinguishing features; Illustrations**

Complete the chart by using the information in Units 25 to 28 and thereby make up your own recognition guide. You will find this very useful for your work in Volume 3 so try to make it as accurate as possible.

Summary

1900 to 1940

1. Built of brick and sometimes decorated with pebbledash; windows side opening.
2. Introduction of council house estates both on the edges of towns and cities and in some villages.
3. Porches around the front door.
4. Coloured glass patterns on the upper half of the front door.
5. Roof tiled.
6. During 1930s many new houses and housing estates built in the south and midlands.
7. Houses built with garages from approximately 1936.

1940 to present day

1. Red-brick houses often with attached garages.
2. Large picture windows.
3. Use of steel and concrete allowed taller buildings with deeper foundations to be built. Therefore, introduction of high flats, especially in areas of limited space.
4. No chimneys on houses with oil, electric or gas central heating.
5. More factory-built materials used.
6. House building greatly increased after World War Two.
7. New houses in villages usually infilling.
8. Modern housing estates in towns are often pedestrian only and cars are parked in a small area set aside for the purpose a little distance away.
9. New buildings of the age which you would not have seen in previous centuries: airports, office-blocks etc. Also the closing down of many village railway stations.

Revision Units 25–28

Building styles

1 Read the following statements dealing with buildings and building styles. Say whether they are true or false and for those that you think are false give reasons for your answer.

(a) Many new castles were built after the year 1600.
(b) The floor beams of the second and third storeys in Tudor houses can usually be seen on the outside of the house.
(c) All early houses in Britain were built using wood.
(d) Georgian houses in London were often built or faced with Portland stone.
(e) Most modern houses are now built on estates.
(f) The practice of building houses on spare plots of land between existing houses in a village is called infilling.
(g) Georgian houses had thatched roofs.
(h) The oldest building in a village is always a public house.
(i) One way of finding out the age of the church is to find the oldest gravestone; however, this is not a very accurate way of doing it.
(j) A 1930s house often had the pattern of the rising sun on the doors, gates and garages.

2 Look very carefully at the following photographs and identify the times in which they were built.

Fig. R1

Fig. R2

Fig. R3

Fig. R4

Unit 29
Introduction to artefacts

29.1 A modern example

If a man came into your house and emptied the contents of his jacket pocket on your table and they included a box of matches, a golf-tee, a railway season-ticket, and two tickets to a local cinema for the same date, what could you say about him? Look at the articles again.

Individually they tell you very little, but if you take them together, you can build up a reasonable picture of the man's lifestyle. For instance, a golf-tee immediately tells you that he probably plays golf; the box of matches may suggest that our character is a smoker, but because he has not put a packet of cigarettes on the table we cannot say that this is definite – it may mean that he needs them for lighting a fire or cooker at home. The railway season-ticket can tell us two things, firstly that he uses a train every day, probably to go to work, and secondly, if our theory is correct, that he lives a train-journey away from his job and is, therefore, not close to it. He also visits the cinema in his free time and on this particular occasion he did not go alone.

Four simple artefacts which on their own would be of little use if you wished to describe your character, but using all of them we can make a reasonable guess, using the available clues, that the man is a golf-playing (tee), commuter (season ticket), who possibly smokes (matches) and enjoys visiting the cinema with a friend (two cinema tickets). By being observant you have built up a very interesting description of this man, and if you included what he wore and how he acted you could add to your first opinion of him.

29.2 The value of artefacts to the historian

Historians have to use artefacts and articles in the same way, but often, of course, they are not only dealing with simple present day ones as we have done in this example, but also artefacts from the past. The main difference is that you could quite easily have found out if your assessment of the man in the example was correct by just asking him. The historian needs to examine an article and work out its use and its age by looking at other clues, either documents or reference books, or certain marks on the artefact itself, in order to place it in its approximate place in history.

Everything has a purpose

But how can the historian use these clues, and what can the artefact actually tell him. Generally you need to remember that all articles that you see around you, like people and places, have a history of their own. Everything has been developed for a certain purpose, even if it was only meant to look pretty on a mantelpiece.

Tracing developments

Unfortunately, artefacts break. Those that do, and those that are no longer of any use or out-of-date or even unfashionable are simply thrown away. This is not a new practice, man has been throwing away his unwanted possessions for thousands of years. We saw in Unit 14 how man needed to improve his weapons and tools in order to catch and kill his food. As soon as an improved 'up-to-date' stone axehead was introduced, the old one was thrown away. When bronze was discovered, man threw all his stone tools on the rubbish heap, and when iron was found the bronze ones joined the pile. The same pattern has been going on ever since. You probably do exactly the same today; when a new style of shoes becomes fashionable, you discard your old ones.

But how do all these cast-offs and rejected artefacts help the historian? Just like the contents of our example pockets these piles or pits of discarded articles, if found, can provide the historian with clues to what people used, wore, fought with or ate in the past. How else would we know that early man used stone weapons or ate meat, if their rubbish piles containing **stone implements** and animal bones had not been found in different parts of the world.

29.3 The archaeologist

The person who does this digging into the past and who carefully examines and lists all the articles that are found is called an archaeologist. An archaeologist was once described as a person who 'makes a scientific study of other people's rubbish', and basically that is what they often do. They make sure that all artefacts that are removed from the ground are carefully catalogued and a record of exactly where they were found is made for future reference. How can these articles be dated? Artefacts such as tools or pottery or weapons have been written about over a number of years and the changes in styles and fashions are easily found in reference books in your local library.

Fig. 29.1 A group of archaeologists at work

29.4 The process of dating

Articles from long ago can be dated scientifically, but there are simple aids which can allow the archaeologist to make a reasonable guess as to the age of a particular artefact found on a **dig**.

Coins

The most common everyday article that people tend to drop, either from their pockets or purses, are coins. Most coins have dates on them, so if you drop a coin dated 1984 in your garden and leave it there, the soil and grass and leaves will gradually cover it. In a few hundred years time an archaeologist digging in the same area will find your coin and because of the date on it, he will know that he has reached a level of approximately 1984. The coin would then be useful in helping to date other artefacts found on the same level of digging. For instance, if the same archaeologist found a badge that had fallen from your jacket in the same level as the coin, he could say that the badge comes from a time around the year 1984.

Coins are so useful to the historian and especially the archaeologist that they are not very happy about people using metal-detectors on archaeological sites just for fun. These people find coins and other metal objects and dig them up, usually without making any note of exactly where they were found. When dug up in this way the coins are no longer useful as an aid to dating other artefacts and material on the site.

Fig. 29.2 An archaeologist sketching a find

Unit 29 continued

Fig. 29.3 The Roman villa at Littlecote House, near Hungerford

Activities

Look at the following diagram of an archaeological dig. Some coins have been found and their dates are clearly seen. Using them as an aid write down the approximate years the other articles were dropped.

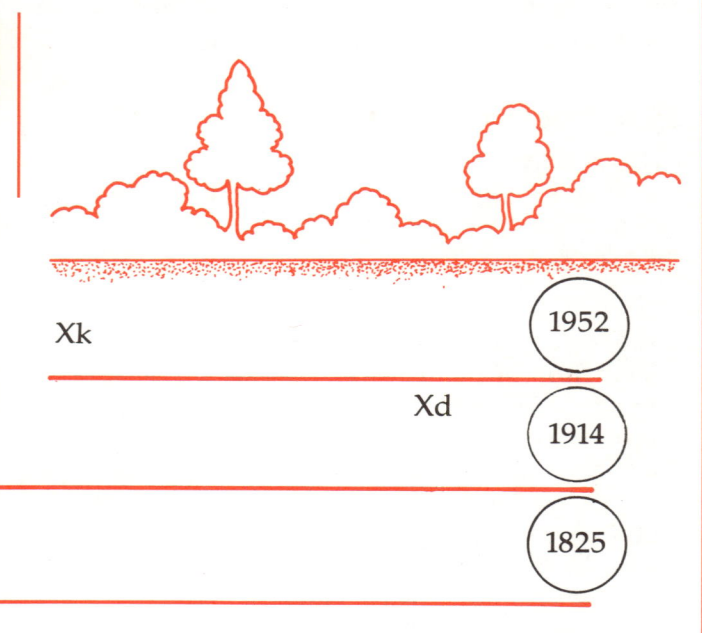

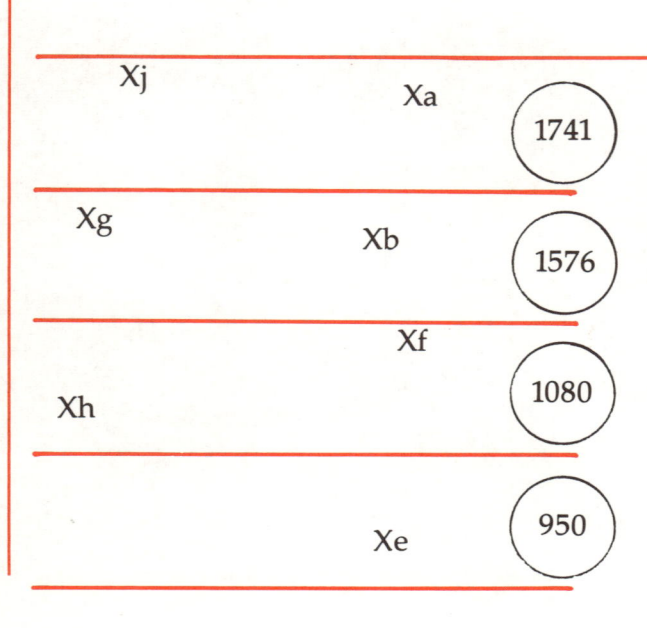

Xk — 1952
Xd — 1914
Xc
1825
Xj
Xa — 1741
Xg
Xb — 1576
Xf
1080
Xh
Xe — 950

Summary

1 Artefacts, like people and places, have their own history.
2 Artefacts can provide the historian with clues about the way of life in the past.
3 A person who digs up, labels, catalogues and examines articles from the past is called an archaeologist.
4 Coins are a useful aid to dating levels of **excavation** on an archaeological **dig**.

Unit 30
More about artefacts

In the previous unit you were introduced to the topic of artefacts and articles and given a simple example of how to use such articles to help you gain information about a particular subject. Our example of the mysterious visitor was set in the present day and it would therefore, be easy to find out if your theories about him were correct by asking him. You were told that historians and archaeologists have to search for articles and often they are unable to support their theories by asking the person or group of people concerned and, therefore, they have to rely on gathering the information they require from facts and knowledge they already have, and from the articles themselves.

Fig. 30.1 What information can you gather about William Mullins' trade?

BASKETMAKING

1 Bat – straightens the ends of the willow
2 Brakes – willow pulled through these to remove bark
2 Knives
4 Signboard
5 Basket stall
6 Template
7 Cleavers – to split willow rods
8 Shave – reducing thickness of willow
9 Upright shave
10 Weight
11 Grease horn – lubricates bodkins
12 Clamp
13 White willow – heavy round basket base
14 White willow – round basket base
15 White willow – demonstration basket
16 Secateurs – cut cane
17 Shears
18 Squeezers
19 Shop or hand knives
20 Bodkins
21 Picking knife – trims ends of rods
22 Shell bodkins – used in repair work
23 Beating irons
24 Commander – straightens or bends thick willow

Unit 30 continued

30.1 Artefacts in museums

Unless you are very lucky, you will be unlikely to experience the delight of digging up some rare archaeological find from the ground, but it is possible for you to see such articles and gain information from them. Most historical artefacts are kept in museums, often in glass cases, but occasionally you will come across some museums which allow you to pick up, handle and examine the less valuable **relics**. Your local museum may even have a section which sends historical artefacts to schools, so if you are interested, it may be worth asking your history teacher if it would be possible to borrow some so that your class could take more time examining them.

30.2 Looking at artefacts

Just looking at these articles can be interesting, but in order to use them as an historian you would need to ask yourself certain questions and write down your answers. You can either write them down in a notebook on the spot, or you could record them on a portable tape-recorder and write down the answers later, when you have more time. The advantage of recording your information on tape is that you can describe the article in more detail in a shorter time than it would take you to write it down, and when you wish to describe more than one article, time is very important.

(Before you use a tape-recorder in a museum always obtain permission and always keep your voice low when speaking into it so as not to disturb other people around you.) If possible try to get a picture of the article. This can be a rough sketch, or a photograph if it is possible to take one, or a picture postcard which you may find on sale in the museum. You will see how these can be used later.

Questions to ask

Having seen or handled the artefact, what questions do you need to ask yourself? First, you need to know what the article is. If you have no definite idea you could look for any label attached to the artefact or look in the display case for a card describing it. If there is no written description of any kind you can ask a member of the museum staff, or if you have the articles at school you can ask your teacher. Having worked out what the article is you need to say what it is made of, and also take a note of its size. Then if possible try to find out its approximate age (again this information may be available to you on a label or card). Do not worry if you cannot find out the age because you may be able to look it up in a reference book at a later date, and, although the date would be useful, it is not absolutely necessary for your first investigation.

Is it genuine?

Next ask yourself what the article may have been used for, and who might have used it. Later, when you have had some practice at this type of study you may like to suggest whether or not a particular article is genuine or perhaps a **replica**. All you need do is to look very carefully at all the information you have gathered so far and see if it seems to be 'true'.

It would, of course, be very difficult for you to work out the truth of some articles, and even the experts get it wrong sometimes, but others could be very easy. For instance if you were shown a Viking helmet said to date from around AD 800 and you noticed that the rivets looked very modern and new you could say that either the article was a replica or that it had been mended at some time using modern materials. You would then have to ask further questions to find out the truth. Another example would be a china plate said to have come from around 1500. Not only were china plates not in common use at this time, but also if they had been, they would have been very lucky to have survived for so long without breaking. An historian would have to examine such an article very carefully before saying that it was genuine.

History comes to life

One interesting part of examining artefacts from the past, and part of the fun of history, is that you can actually say that once upon a time a Roman soldier held this sword, or once a cavalier wore this hat, or a duchess sat in this chair. With a little thought you can actually imagine yourself back in those times and put yourself in the place of the original owner of the artefact you are holding.

30.3 Recording the information

When you have asked yourself all the relevant questions and either written down or recorded your answers, you now need to have some way of storing all the information you have gathered. If you intend listing a lot of articles it may be useful to collect the information on filing cards and store them in a small box or index file. (These are easily obtainable from large stationers or newsagents.) You need to divide your cards into sections, as in Fig. 30.2. Each artefact will have a separate card, so all you need do is complete it with the answers to the questions. If you have a picture of the article you can attach it to its card to help you with future reference.

ARTICLE: *Household Iron*
DATE SEEN: *25 March 1984*
PLACE SEEN: *County Museum*

DESCRIPTION OF ARTICLE
Material *Iron*
Size *Approx 12cm long, 8cm wide*
Smell (if any) *Metallic*
What is/was it used for? *Ironing clothes*
Who may have used it? *A housewife, or, in a wealthy household, the maid*
Approx how old? AD *1900*
Country of origin *England*
Other details *Foundry name 'Siddons'*

Fig. 30.2 A record card

You may also like to add two things that were happening at the same time as this article was in use: the Boer War, and the last full year of Queen Victoria's reign. Also you may wish to add the question '**what other information do I need to find out about this article?**'.

Filing system

When you have collected a number of these cards you need to have some method of filing them in your box so that you can easily find them at a later date. You can either do this alphabetically, (see page 75) or perhaps by article. For instance you could have a section on household goods, or weapons, or pottery articles. You can make up your own system to suit your own purpose. Remember that the system must allow you to find or retrieve the information quickly without having to search through all the cards in the box.

Activities

Before you go out to museums or to look at artefacts at school, search through your shed or cupboard at home and practise your questions and the recording of your answers. If you come across something particularly interesting you may wish to record it on a file card.

Summary

1 When handling and examining articles you need to ask yourself the following questions:
(a) What is it?
(b) What is it made of?
(c) How big is it?
(d) How old is it?
(e) What was it used for?
(f) Who might have used it?
(g) Is it genuine?

2 Information to help answer these questions can often be found on labels or cards attached to the article.

3 Record your answers either in a notebook or on a portable tape recorder. It is courteous to obtain permission before you use a recorder in a museum, and if you do use one remember to keep your voice down.

4 Keep all this information on individual cards and store them in an index file.

5 Work out your own filing system which allows you to retrieve the information you require quickly and easily.

6 Whenever possible attach a picture of the article to the card describing it.

Unit 31

Collecting artefacts: an historical hobby

In Unit 30 we talked about artefacts that you can see and possibly examine in a museum, and looked at a simple method of storing the information you could gather from such an investigation. It was also suggested that you might like to look through your own household artefacts or your grandparents' (with their permission) and see what things you could find that may be of interest to you.

31.1 The value of collections

If you want a simpler place to begin you could even start with yourself! Do you collect anything? Do you keep old copies of comics or magazines? Do you buy all the latest fashions and throw the out-of-date ones to the back of your cupboard? If you are a collector or **hoarder**, the sort of person who cannot throw anything away, you could be very useful to historians in the future.

If your collection is found or sold by a member of your family, not only would it be of interest as a collection, but it would also give the historian some idea of what life is like today. For instance, a collection of comics from today would tell him or her the type of things which interested the youth of this period and if they contain fashion pages or sports pages it would give an idea of the general interests of the population. As we said in Unit 30, all artefacts have their own history, they were made or painted or drawn for some specific purpose, and some of these items from the past have become very collectable, and in some cases very valuable, because there may be few examples left.

This type of collecting can be very interesting to you as an historian because if you treat each article in the same way as those on view in a museum and write up the same sort of index card, changing the words 'Place seen' to 'Place bought' you could then find out as much as possible about the articles and could quite easily become very knowledgable about them.

Small collections can easily grow

Large collections built up and gathered over a number of years are worth seeing and they are often a feature of a visit to a large historical house. For instance, if you visit Littlecote House near Hungerford in Berkshire not only will you see a very large collection of Parliamentary Civil War uniforms and weapons dating from 1644 to 1646 hanging from the walls of the Great Hall, but you will also see a collection of china milk-jugs in the shape of cows, and of Italian glass paper-weights. If you are a collector and see huge collections such as these, it usually encourages you to make yours bigger.

Fig. 31.1 'Animals of the Countryside': a collection of cigarette cards

31.2 Choosing a subject

Where do you start collecting? You certainly cannot go to your local museum and offer to buy some of their artefacts. If you tried the exercise in Unit 30 you, in fact, have started at the best place. Your old toys and especially your parents' toys are very collectable. Remember that a lot of toys reflect what is going on in the 'grown-ups' world at the time, so a model car of 1948 is a model of a car that you would have seen being driven along the road if you had lived at the time. A doll's pram was often a miniature version of a real baby's pram and dolls were often clothed in the fashion of the time.

Once you have searched all the nooks and crannies in your house where do you continue? To make your searching, and your collecting easier it is worth concentrating on only one or two types of artefact, especially if you wish to become an 'expert' – you will not have to read so much!

Before you decide what to collect, remember that modern articles such as badges or tee-shirts will be very easy to find, but will have very little historical value for you, only to someone in the future. Decide upon something simple which can be collected from the past and which is inexpensive, for example, picture postcards. This is an interesting subject to study and collect because it is possible to see the changes in a seaside resort by looking at the pictures of it on the postcards. (Remember the witting and unwitting testimony in Unit 16.)

31.3 Finding items for your collection

Where do you find them? Most towns and some villages have **antique shops**. It is worth looking in these shops not only for your postcards but also to see some of the artefacts from the past. You can get a good idea of the type of furniture people had in their houses or the type of cutlery they used or the style of kitchen equipment they had. Antique shops are almost history shops dealing with the daily lives of people in the past. Sometimes a group of antique dealers get together in a local hall and have an **antique fair**. When you are looking around these shops or fairs be very careful not to knock over a priceless vase! If you do not like the idea of going into antique shops or fairs, look out for advertisements in your local newspaper referring to **car-boot sales** or even **jumble sales**. Most articles on sale are often very cheap and it is possible to find some bargains.

31.4 Recording information on your collection

In order to use your collection as an historical exercise we have said that you will need to obtain as much information about the articles as possible. You will, therefore, need access to a local library or school library because the reference books you will need are often very expensive.

Fig. 31.2 A delightful example of an old postcard

With some articles it is useful to have some idea of the date it was made so that you are able to see the changes in the style over a period of time (this will be dealt with more fully in Volume 2). If you are able to find out the date, it will be possible to file your index cards in **chronological order** i.e. year by year.

Hallmarks

Some articles have clues to their ages on them, especially gold, silver and chinaware. Each genuine piece of gold and silver has a **hallmark** stamped on it.

From the Middle Ages goldsmiths and silversmiths (men who worked with gold and silver) have had to have their work checked and inspected to make sure they have the correct amount of the metal in them. If correct, the articles are stamped to show that they are of good quality. The hallmark symbols show the town in which it was tested, the maker's initials, and, most important from your point of view, the date it was tested. It would be impossible to write down all the examples of possible hallmarks, so if you decide to try the expensive business of collecting silver articles it would be worth buying a pocket-sized reference book containing all the hallmarks and explanations of them.

Makers' names

Chinaware usually has the maker's name stamped on the bottom of the article. Some of these stamps and signs change so the date of the article can often be worked out from the changes in symbol. These can be found in a book dealing with china marks.

Whatever articles you finally decide to collect, enjoy collecting them, and remember you are collecting part of history.

Unit 31 continued

Activities

1 Imagine that while walking along a road you find a lady's handbag lying on the pavement. The bag contains the following articles. Look at them carefully and use the available clues to describe the lady who owns this bag.

(a) Library ticket from Putney Library. The name on the ticket is Jane Smith.
(b) Old ticket for a Beethoven concert at the Royal Albert Hall.
(c) A Pitmans Bank cheque book with the names Jane and Paul Smith on the cheques.
(d) A set of car keys on a Ford key ring.
(e) A packet of peppermints.
(f) A tube of sweeteners.
(g) A child allowance book with the name Jane Smith and an address.
(h) A programme of events for the Putney branch of the Women's Institute.

2 How could you return this bag to its owner?

3 Look very carefully at the following photograph of a Roman floor tile. Apart from showing you what a Roman floor looks like, what other information can this particular tile provide you with?

Fig. 31.3 A Roman floor tile

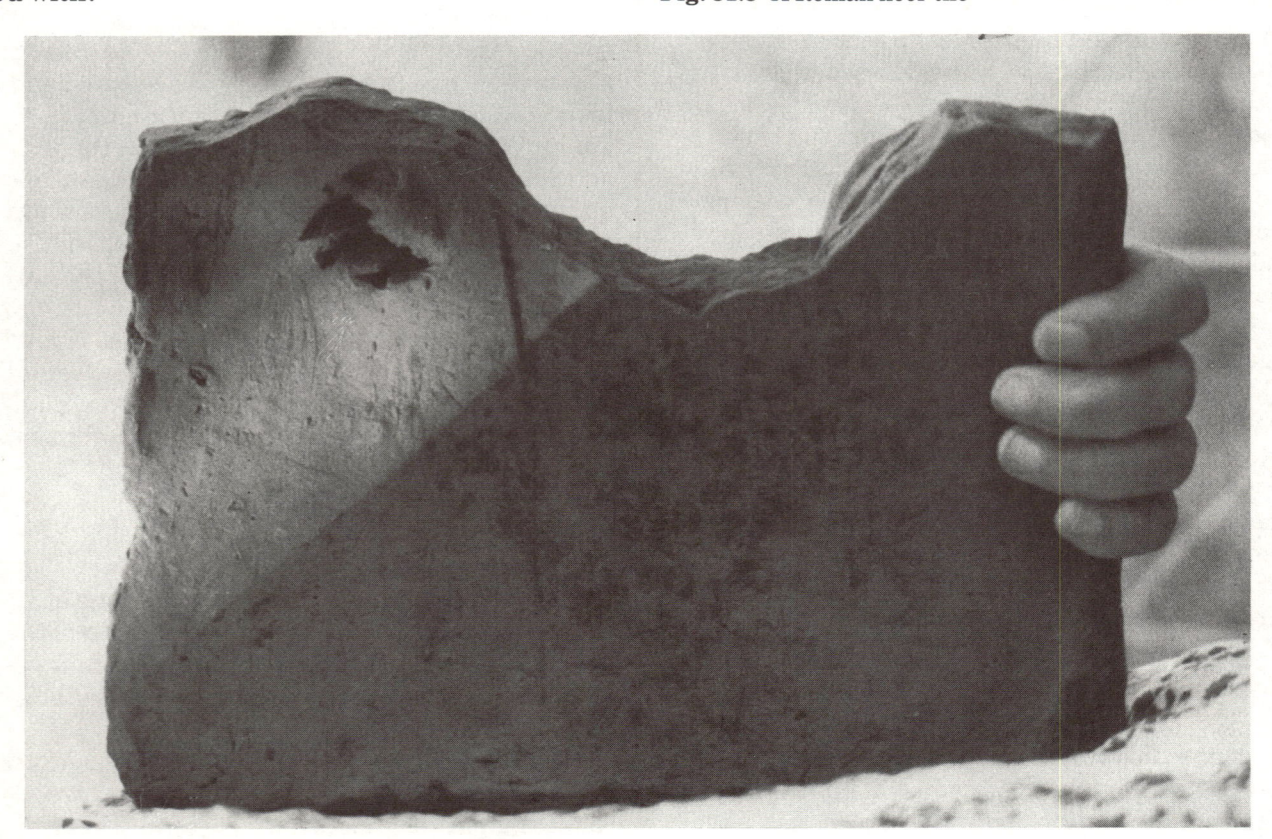

4 You are working on an archaeological dig and you find a number of British coins. Unfortunately all the dates on the coins have been worn away, but you can still see the head of the king or queen quite clearly. You need the coins to give an approximate date to the level you found them in. Using the information available, write down the years between which the coins could have been dropped. Remember that the coins would not have been used before the particular monarch came to the throne i.e. coins from the reign of Queen Elizabeth II were not **minted** until 1952, but they will be in use for many years to come, even during the reign of the next monarch. Therefore, you, as an archaeologist, could only say for certain that the level you had reached in your dig could not have been laid down before 1952.

The coins show the following kings and queens:

Charles I	**Elizabeth I**
Queen Victoria	**George II**
James II	**Queen Anne**
Edward VI	**George III**
George V	**Elizabeth II**
William IV	**Henry VII**

When you have the dates, draw a sketch of the dig showing where they may have been found. Remember that the most recent coin would be found nearest the surface.

Summary

1 If you decide to start a collection, use it as an historical study.
2 Only collect one or two types of article.
3 Read about the artefacts you collect and try to become an expert on them.
4 All genuine articles made from gold and silver have a hallmark. This will give you the place and date the article was tested or **assayed**.

Fig. 31.4 Hallmarks on old silver

Unit 32

Secondary sources

In the past few units we have looked closely at some primary sources of information available to you as an historian. These have included documents, photographs, diaries, letters and events you have witnessed yourself and artefacts you may have found or examined.

Primary sources of information are those in their original or **prime** form. Secondary sources are different. They are simply sources which provide the historian with the facts second-hand.

32.1 Examples of secondary sources

Example 1

Jane finds an old letter in a box at home. She reads it and because it interests her, she writes down the information contained in it in her own words. Sally needs such a letter to help her with her history homework and asks Jane if she may use it. Jane decides not to let Sally use the original letter because she does not want it to get lost, but she does allow her to use her own copy.

PRIMARY SOURCE

Jane

Jane finds letter . . .

copies information contained in letter in her own words

SECONDARY SOURCE

Sally needs letter for her history homework

Second hand information

Sally

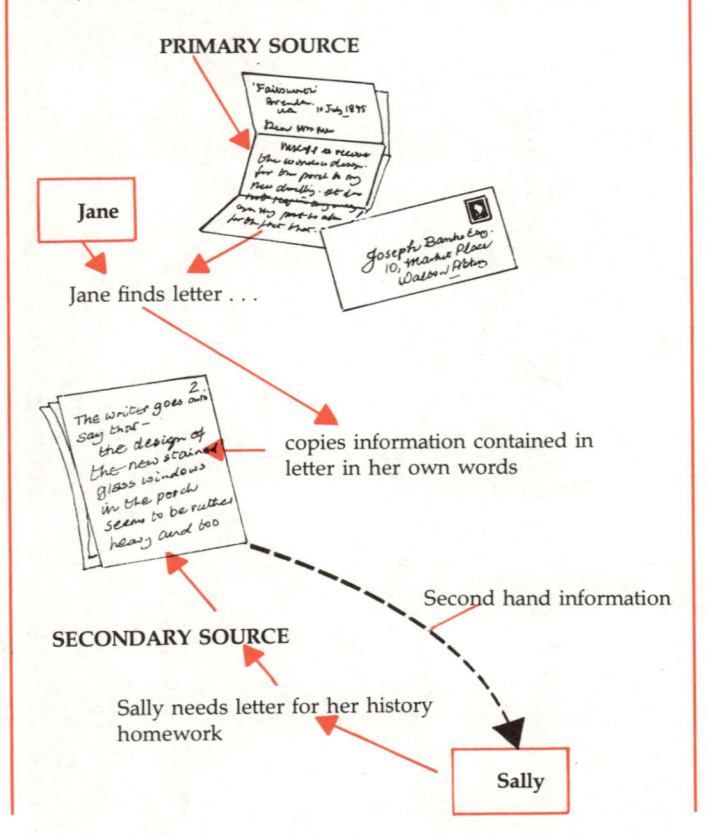

Remember, although the information contained in this copy is the same as in the letter, it is not in the same words. Jane could have changed the original meaning very slightly in some way by not writing it down exactly. By borrowing Jane's copy, Sally is now receiving the information from the letter second-hand. This copy is a secondary source of information because it is not in its original or prime condition.

Example 2

Look at the following extracts from a diary; imagine it was written by one of your family and you find it during a search of your cupboard.

(a) '4 January 1947. Weather still very cold. Snowy conditions outside. Water pipes frozen inside. No more coal, will have to queue at the coal yard again tomorrow.'

This is a primary source. It is a diary extract giving the historian a description of the weather and conditions during the harsh winter of 1947. It would have been written by someone who was actually there at the time.

During one of your modern history lessons at school you are asked to write a short description of the problems faced by the people living through the winter of 1947. You remember that you have your relative's diary extract at home and you decide to use it to provide you with some of the information needed in your work. Your final answer contains the following passage based on the diary extract:

(b) 'The winter of 1947 was an extremely cold one. Not only were the weather conditions bad outdoors with snowdrifts and ice, but many people suffered from frozen pipes indoors, often because they did not have enough coal to keep their houses warm. Coal was in short supply and in order to get any, people would have to queue for long hours at a local coal yard. . .'

The information in example 2(a), the primary source, has been used to help you answer your question about 1947. You would naturally write your answer in your own words, but notice that by doing so you have guessed some facts about the conditions. For example, were 'snowdrifts' mentioned in example 2(a)? How did you know that people had to queue 'for long hours' or that the lack of coal caused the frozen pipes? You have assumed that all these things occurred, and from the information available in example 2.(a) they are reasonable **assumptions**. But the facts are no longer in their original form. Example 2.(b) is now a secondary source. Anyone wishing to use example 2.(b) to collect facts about 1947 will read not the original diary, but your **interpretation** of the facts contained in it. They would be using a second-hand source.

The simple diagram below may help you understand the two examples a little more easily.

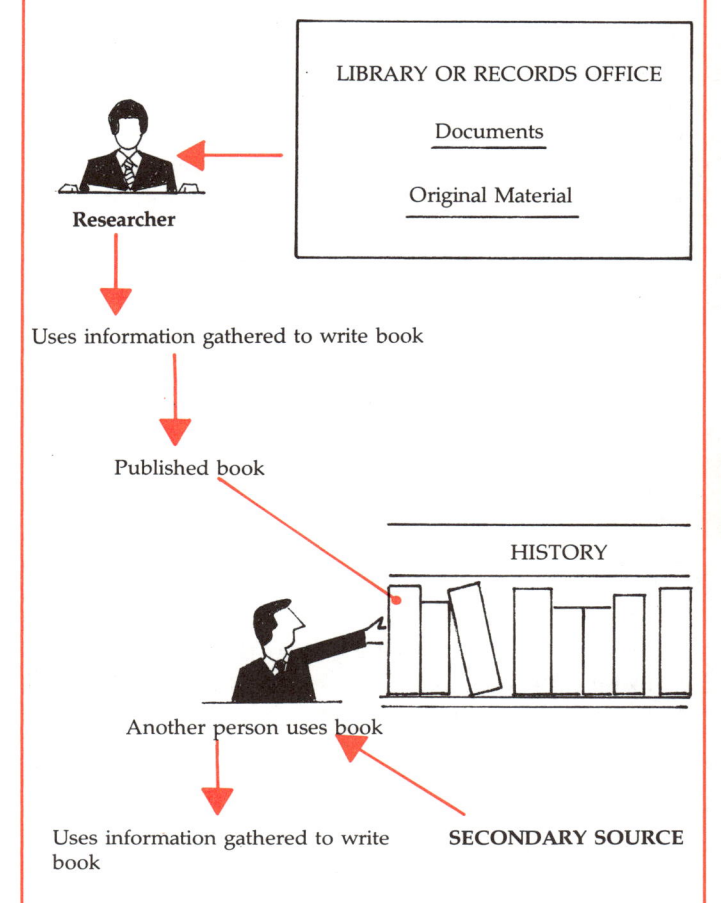

```
Researcher  ←  LIBRARY OR RECORDS OFFICE
                    Documents
                    Original Material
    ↓
Uses information gathered to write book
    ↓
Published book
    ↓
Another person uses book → HISTORY (SECONDARY SOURCE)
    ↓
Uses information gathered to write book
```

1 Jane finds a letter (primary source) and takes notes from it. Sally borrows Jane's notes from this letter to help with her homework — Sally is therefore using the material second-hand. It is not in prime condition i.e. the original letter. She is using Jane's notes of the contents.

2 DIARY EXTRACT = PRIMARY SOURCE... INFORMATION IN EXTRACT REWRITTEN AND USED... ANSWER USED BY ANOTHER PERSON... TO HELP ANSWER QUESTION. NOW A SECONDARY SOURCE.

32.2 History books

Many of the history books you are likely to come across at school will be secondary sources. The authors have researched from the original material and documents (primary sources) and have interpreted and rewritten the information contained in them in a way the reader will understand. When you use the information they have already gathered you are therefore using it second-hand. Authors, of course, use secondary as well as primary material. They also read around the subject and see what other people have found out about the subject before them. Usually you will find a list of these sources in the back of a text book or sometimes in the front where it says **acknowledgements**.

32.3 Other secondary sources

We will study history books in more detail in Units 33 and 34. Other secondary sources include: school text books, history journals, history papers, newspapers and biographies (the life history of a person written by someone else). All these examples have information in them which has been gathered from primary and other secondary sources and which you are reading second-hand.

Activities

Which of the following are primary sources and which are secondary?

1 An entry in a personal diary kept by a cricketer in the Test series against the West Indies in 1984.

2 A collection of artefacts from the archaeological dig at Littlecote House.

3 A fashion editor's description of the fashions in the 1950s.

4 A newspaper article describing the events of the England v West Indies Test Cricket series in 1984.

5 An historical paper written on the subject of the archaeological dig at Littlecote House.

6 A photograph of a group of models displaying the fashions of the 1950s.

Summary

1 All information available first hand is a **primary** source.

2 All information gathered from someone else's work, and so gained second-hand, is a **secondary** source.

3 If you use information from a school text-book or newspaper, you will in most cases be using a secondary source.

4 Changes can be made in the writing down of information from primary sources. So secondary sources contain the authors' interpretation of the facts collected from primary sources.

Unit 33
Libraries

History books are an important tool of the historian, but, unfortunately, these are often very expensive to buy, so it is very convenient to borrow the books you require from your local or school library, at no cost at all.

The problem is how to find the book you need among the many that are on the shelves. In your school library you may have a simple method of sorting out the books. Sometimes they have small labels on their spines showing what they contain, for example, a picture of a ghost means that the book contains 'ghost stories' or a magnifying glass shows that it is a 'detective novel'. But although this may be useful for story books in a small library, it is not very helpful in a large library containing fiction and non-fiction books. So how do you find the book you require in a large library?

33.1 Sections of the library

Reference section

A library is divided up into many sections, each containing the same type of book, very similar to the way in which the same sort of food is put in the same section of shelves in your local supermarket. The type of book you need will depend on how much detailed information you require. If you wish to find out some general knowledge about a certain historical event you could look first in the section marked **General reference**. This section usually contains **dictionaries** and **encyclopaedias**, which can be referred to in order to find the facts you need. If, for example, you were asked a question about the date of the Gunpowder Plot you would find the answer more quickly by looking it up, in an encyclopaedia than by looking through all the relevant books in the history section. Usually an encyclopaedia comprises (contains) many different books called volumes. The initial letter of the subjects contained in each volume is marked on the spine. All the entries are listed in **alphabetical order** (see Unit 23), so to find out about the Gunpowder Plot you would look for the volume containing all the subjects starting with the letter G and find the entry under Gunpowder Plot. Remember, you cannot take reference books out of the library, you may only use them, or refer to them, in the building. However, you should be able to get all the facts you need very quickly because reference books are not meant to be read from cover to cover and the titles of the subjects are easily found.

Classified sections

But how would you find out more detailed information about the Gunpowder Plot? If you wanted to find a story, or fiction book on a library shelf you would find that it would be sorted in alphabetical order according to the author's surname. Non-fiction books are **classified** in a different way. They are arranged on the shelves according to the subject matter they contain. They are **not** classified in alphabetical order.

Many libraries use a classification method known as the **Dewey decimal classification system** named after an American named Melvin Dewey who divided all knowledge into **ten** parts. This method of classification uses numbers and they can be found on the spines of all non-fiction books, and on the corresponding shelves which contain them. They range from 000 to 999. The numbers you, as an historian, would be interested in are the **900s**. This classification number covers history, geography and biography. Each of the ten main parts 000 to 999 is divided again into ten further parts, so the 900s would be divided into 910 to 990 and cover the information as follows:

900 = Geography, biography and history
910 = Ancient history and archaeology
920 = Biography
930 = General history of the ancient world
940 = European history
950 = General history of Asia
960 = General history of Africa
970 = North American history
980 = General history of South America
990 = General history of other parts of the world

Sub-divisions

Sometimes you will find a decimal point and then another number after the main one which helps to classify the books in even more detail. As you can see from the above list, if you were interested in the general history of Europe, you would look for a book with the number 940 on its spine, but because the history of Europe is such a large area to study it is 'sub-divided' even further, for example:

940.1 = The history of Medieval Europe 476 to AD 1453
940.2 = The history of Europe from 1453 to 1914
940.3 = The causes of the First World War
940.4 = The military history of World War One
940.5 = The history of 20th century Europe

The history of 20th-century Europe is a large topic, so 940.5 can be sub-divided again to cover the main historical events in the century:

940.53 = The history of World War Two
940.54 = The military history of World War Two
940.55 = The history of Europe since World War Two

Therefore, if you needed a book on the D-Day Landings of 1944 you would look for a classification number of 940.54: **900** = History, **940** = European history. **940.5** = European history in the 20th century and 940.54 = The military history of World War Two.

A combination of sections

Of course, it is possible to find the information you need from more than one book under more than one classification. So if you wanted to find out more about Guy Fawkes and the Gunpowder Plot you could look at the books with the number 942 for British history, (940 = European history, 942 the British section of European history) and also at the books numbered 920 for Biography where you may find a book giving you the life history of Guy Fawkes.

Below is a list of useful 'Dewey' numbers which may help you when you are dealing with a particular topic. Remember, these numbers can be sub-divided even further.

355 = Military history
391 = Costume
560 = Prehistoric life e.g. fossils, dinosaurs
720 = Architecture
728 = Castles
932 = Ancient Egypt
937 = Ancient Rome
938 = Ancient Greece
940.3/4 = World War One
940.53/4 = World War Two

33.2 The library catalogue

All books in any library can be found by using the library's catalogue. We saw in Unit 23 how to find references to documents in the records' office by looking through the index file and, similarly, you find available library books by looking through the library catalogue. This catalogue is not a coloured brochure like those which occasionally come through your letter box advertising articles for sale, but usually a number of drawers in a cabinet which contain a card for each book in the library. (In some larger libraries the information from the catalogue cards has been photographed on microfilm in order to save space.)

Uses of the catalogue: subject index

A library catalogue can be useful to you in two ways. Imagine you are searching for more detailed information about the Gunpowder Plot and you do not know which books may contain the facts you need. You would go to the catalogue drawer marked **subject index** and find the subject heading Gunpowder Plot. These subject cards are stored in alphabetical order. The card you will find will be similar to this one:

GUNPOWDER PLOT: BRITISH HISTORY: 942.061

The card tells you the Dewey classification number for the group of books dealing with this subject. You would then look up this number in the **classified catalogue** and find cards which will give you all the titles of the books in that particular library which contain information about the Gunpowder Plot. Here is an example of such a card:

942.061 . . . . Dewey Number

Author's Name . . . . Winstock, L.

Title . . . . Gunpowder Treason and Plot

Publisher . . . . Wayland

Yr. of Publication 1973

Unit 33 continued

This card would be found in the classified catalogue under the number 942.061 in the section marked 'W'.

Having found the card and read all the information on it you could then find this particular book on the shelf marked with the same classification number.

Uses of the catalogue: authors' index

The other way in which the library catalogue could be of use to you is if you already know that L. Winstock has written a book about the Gunpowder Plot and you want to see if the library has it. You would look at all the cards under Winstock, L in the authors' catalogue and find the card containing the information about the subject you require. The card will be an exact copy of the previous example which we found in the classified catalogue. All cards in the authors' catalogue are stored in alphabetical order according to surname.

Summing up the procedure

You would use the same routine when searching for any non-fiction book you wish to see: if you know the authors' name, find the relevant card, and, therefore, the classification number in the authors' index. If, however, you only know the subject, find the card referring to that subject in the subject index and read off the 'Dewey' number, then look for a card or cards with this same number in the classified catalogue. You will then find information on all the books in the library dealing with that particular topic. Once you have the number for the books, you look for it on the shelf with the same number.

33.3 Will the book be suitable?

Having found the book, how do you know it will be suitable for your study? Of course if the title of the book mentions the subject you are interested in, it is certain to contain some of the facts you require. For instance, you would not look at a book with the title *'The Development of Horse Transport'* and expect it to give you information about the history of costume. But some books contain many pages and a great deal of information, so how do you know, even if it has the correct title, that the book you have picked from the shelf is suitable?

First of all you can read the publisher's description on the **fly-leaf** of the dust jacket, if the book has one. This will give you a very brief summary of the subject of the book. Another way is to look at the **contents pages** at the front of the book. Contents are usually very useful because it is possible to find out the subject matter of the whole book just by reading the contents pages. Therefore, the first thing to do when you find a book you think may be suitable is to read the contents pages thoroughly. You could save yourself a lot of time.

33.4 Using the index

Now you know that this book is suitable, how do you find the individual facts you require? In order to do this you need to look at (consult) the index. There is one at the back of most non-fiction books. Each person, place, fact or subject mentioned in the text of the book is found listed in alphabetical order, and alongside each entry you will find a number, or group of numbers, which refer to the pages on which that subject can be found, for example:

advertising posters, 151–2

agriculture, 111; number of farmers in UK 122; women employed in, 212, 290–92; wage increases, 271

aircraft, development of, 32–3

air raids & air raid precautions, 37, 44, 136–7, casualties in UK 197–8

air transport, 308–9

Sub-divisions

You can see from this example that some of the entries in the list are sub-divided into more references. If you were interested in the subject of agriculture, you would know from the above that it is mentioned generally on page 111, but if you wanted to find out about the number of women employed in the industry you would need to look at pages 212, 290–92. You would not have to read the other pages listed under agriculture which would not be relevant to your study.

Activities

For this exercise you will need to visit your nearest library. Below you will find a list of sixteen popular history books which are available in most libraries. You are given all the information about the books except the Dewey Classification Number, and that is what you have to find. (Your answers may differ very slightly from the ones at the back of this book because some libraries may use a different system.)

1 SCOTT A.

One Day in Regency England

TYNDALL 1974

2 HODGES C.W.

Magna Carta

OXFORD UNIVERSITY PRESS 1966

3 CRUSH M.

A First Look at Costume

F. WATTS 1972

4 SCHOFIELD A.

Clothes in History

WAYLAND 1974

5 MILLARD A.

Egyptians

MACDONALD 1975

6 UNSTEAD R.J.

Living in Pompeii

A & C BLACK

7 TAYLOR B.

Picture reference book of The Saxons, Vikings and Normans

BROCKHAMPTON 1968

8 PLUCKROSE H.

Medieval Britain

MILLS & BOON 1980

9 DENNEY N. and J. FILMER-SANKEY

Bayeux Tapestry

COLLINS 1966

10 UNSTEAD R.J.

Tudors & Stuarts

BLACK 1974

11 TRIGGS T.D.

The Saxons

MACDONALD 1976

12 LOYN H.

Norman Britain

LUTTERWORTH PRESS 1966

13 BAILEY M.

Medieval Life

LONGMAN 1972

14 CHAMBERLAIN E.R.

Everyday Life in the 19th Century

MACDONALD 1983

15 UNSTEAD R.J.

Queen Anne to Queen Elizabeth II

BLACK 1969

16 MACAULAY D.

Castle

COLLINS 1977

Summary

1 Encyclopaedias and dictionaries can be found in the General reference section of a library.

2 Reference books such as these can provide you with limited information which can usually be found quickly. All facts are listed in alphabetical order.

3 Fiction books are stored on the shelves in alphabetical order according to the author's surname.

4 Non-fiction books are stored according to **subject**.

5 Non-fiction books are usually classified using the **Dewey decimal system**.

6 History books are found between the numbers 900 to 999, but other information can be found in different sections. (Other useful numbers are given in the text.)

7 All books in a library can be found by using the library's catalogue.

8 You can find the information in two ways:

(a) If you know the subject you wish to study, but not the author, you would search in the **subject index**. The card would give you the Dewey number and you would then find a card with this number in the classified catalogue.

(b) If you know the author and wish to know which books written by him or her are available in the library, you would find the information on the cards in the authors' index – under the author's surname.

9 There are two ways in which you can find out if the book you have chosen is suitable for your topic.

(a) Read through the contents pages at the beginning of the book.

(b) Read the information on the fly-leaf of the dust jacket.

Both ways can save you a lot of time.

10 To find the reference to individual facts you would consult the index at the back of the book, where the page numbers for all the places, people and facts mentioned in the text can be found.

Unit 34
History books

34.1 The problem of bias

History books are extremely important to any historian working on any form of study. We have seen that primary source material is gathered by the historian and written down in his or her own words. The important thing to remember, therefore, when using any history book is that you are reading the author's interpretation of the facts and information available to him. This interpretation or opinion may be very one-sided or biased, so, whenever possible, it is useful to read as many books on the same subject by as many different authors as you can. You will find that some authors are more biased than others, and some may actually disagree with each other; by reading more than one account you should obtain a more balanced opinion.

For example, a book dealing with the Spanish Armada of 1588 written by a Spaniard, or even a Catholic may well be different from either an English or Protestant historian's view of the same event. This is because, in 1588, the Spanish Catholics were hoping to invade Protestant England, and English and Spanish historians may interpret the facts in a different way or see the Armada from completely different points of view. In the same way an English account of the Falklands War in 1982 would probably be very different from an Argentinian one. You may like to think of other written sources where simple bias may be found. (What about the programme notes of your local football team? What do they usually say about the opposition?)

34.2 Different types of history book

There are many types of history book covering a great number of topics. There are too many to discuss on their own, but we will group a few simple examples together and look at them more closely.

On library shelves you will find history books to suit all ages. Some of those available for young readers, or those who have difficulty with reading, contain a lot of pictures and a very small amount of writing, or **text**. The writing is normally printed in large letters so that it can be read easily. If you have problems with reading, or you have a younger brother or sister who may be interested in reading simple history books, these are the ones you should get. You can often obtain as much useful information from the pictures in this type of book as from the text. If, however, you require more facts, and you are able to read well, you will find these books are rather limited.

34.3 Choosing the right books

The type of book you choose will depend entirely on the topic you are studying. Therefore, let us use a previous example again and imagine you wish to study the subject of Guy Fawkes and the Gunpowder Plot. Which books could you use to help you?

Background reading

Before you start reading about any particular historical subject it is always worth knowing something about what else was going on in the country at the same time. By doing this you may be able to understand a little better why the Gunpowder Plot was attempted, and why there were differences between the Catholics and the Protestants at this time in history (1605). You could obtain this wider knowledge by reading the part of a book on the Stuarts dealing with King James I. The King was the plotters' main target. A book such as this will mention the plot, but will also give you a description of James as King and of the problems facing the country at the time. If you wanted a short description of James I or Guy Fawkes or the Gunpowder Plot you could find the information in an encyclopaedia. (Topics are normally listed in alphabetical order.)

GENERAL → The Stuarts
GENERAL → 17th century Britain

SPECIALIST → Encyclopaedias
SPECIALIST → Biographies
SPECIALIST → Subject – Gunpowder plot, etc.

Gunpowder, Treason and Plot
Lettice Cooper

Gunpowder Treason:
A Story of the Gunpowder Plot
Margaret J. Miller

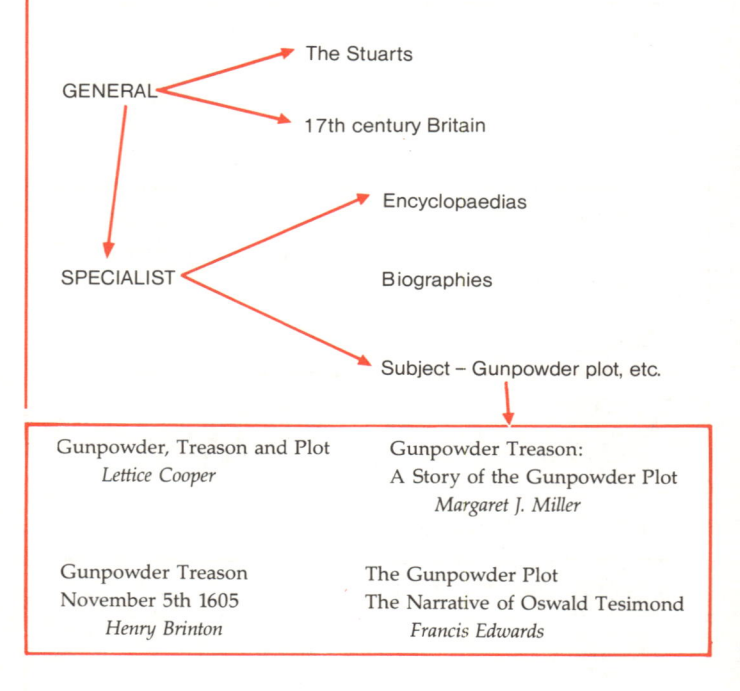

Gunpowder Treason
November 5th 1605
Henry Brinton

The Gunpowder Plot
The Narrative of Oswald Tesimond
Francis Edwards

Fig. 34.1 Flow diagram showing available sources for information on the Gunpowder Plot

Specialized reading

Having read 'around' the subject you would now need to specialize. There are a number of ways to do this, but the simplest, from your point of view, would be to find and read a book written only about the Gunpowder Plot, for example, L. Winstock, *Gunpowder, Treason and Plot* (Unit 33). The author will study the subject in a very detailed way so you would be able to gain a lot of worthwhile information. The subject we have chosen is a very popular one with historians so you will probably find many books written about it. You can choose the one which you will find most interesting to read. Usually there is a short description of what the book contains on the inside flap of the dust cover. If you read this summary it may help you to choose the best one for your purposes.

Biographical reading

The other way to find out about the subject is to use books dealing with the characters involved in the plot in one way or another. This type of book is called a **biography**. For example, you could read books on the life story of Guy Fawkes himself or Sir Francis Walsingham (who was the chief minister of James I), or Robert Catesby, the leader of the plotters, or any other member of the group. You could also read **autobiographies**, the story of the person written by him/herself. You would be unlikely to find any autobiographies written by those involved in the Gunpowder Plot, but they can be very important in other studies. They are a very useful source of information about politicians and high-ranking servicemen who often write their **memoirs** after their retirement. Do not forget that biographies and, especially autobiographies can be as biased or one-sided as any other form of history book and it is always worth while reading someone else's book on the same subject to get a second opinion.

So, for our example we could look at three types of book in order to gather as much information as possible:

A general history e.g. *The Stuarts* – to gain a wider knowledge of what was going on in the country at the time.

A specialist history book e.g. *The Gunpowder Plot* – to gain more specific information about the Gunpowder Plot itself.

Biographies e.g. *Guy Fawkes* – to give you the historical facts about the life of Guy Fawkes. Other biographies could be read in order to find out about others who took part.

Historical novels

As we saw in Unit 33 you will find all these books on the **non-fiction** (not stories) shelves in your library. Sometimes you will see books on the **fiction** or story shelves dealing with historical topics. These books are called 'historical novels'. They are of very little value to you as an historian because they are only stories. Although they may be based on an historical event they contain little historical fact.

Activities

Imagine you have been asked to do a history project on the Spanish Armada of 1588. Which of the following books would you use to help you with your study? Before you tackle this question you may need to find out the main characters who were involved. Queen Elizabeth I and Sir Francis Drake were two of them, but there were many more.

Books available to you

The Spanish Armada, J. SMITH
Philip II of Spain 1527–1598, G. PEREZ
The Duke of Medina Sidonia, T. FLEMING
The Spanish Armada, P. SANCHEZ
The English Civil War, R. ESSEX
Sir Francis Drake, his life and times, D. RALEIGH
Henry VIII, a biography, R. PERCY
The Elizabethan Age, P. KNUTT
The Sea-dogs of Elizabethan times, C. HOARSE

(NB These titles and authors have been made up for the exercise, you will not find them in a library.)

Summary

1 Most history books contain secondary source material.

2 A history book is the author's interpretation of the facts. Therefore history books can be biased.

3 It is always worth reading 'around' a topic before looking at a specialized book on the subject.

4 Biographies and autobiographies can be a useful source of information, but remember they can also be biased.

5 Historical novels, although sometimes enjoyable to read as stories, are of little use to the historian because they contain few historical facts.

Unit 35

Local newspapers

35.1 History as it happens

In Unit 34 we looked at ways in which you can use different types of history books to give you the information you might require for a particular topic. These books could be obtained from your local library or, of course, you could buy them (but remember that some of them can be very costly). There is, however, a very simple 'historical' booklet which you may have delivered to your house every day – a newspaper. By the time the newspaper drops through your letter-box the events you are reading about have already happened and so are in the past and, therefore, history. Newspapers give you an account of day-to-day history almost as it happens. They cover a wide range of topics, and facts can be gathered from the photographs, sports pages, money pages, current affairs and even sometimes the advertisements and of course the letters (see Unit 21).

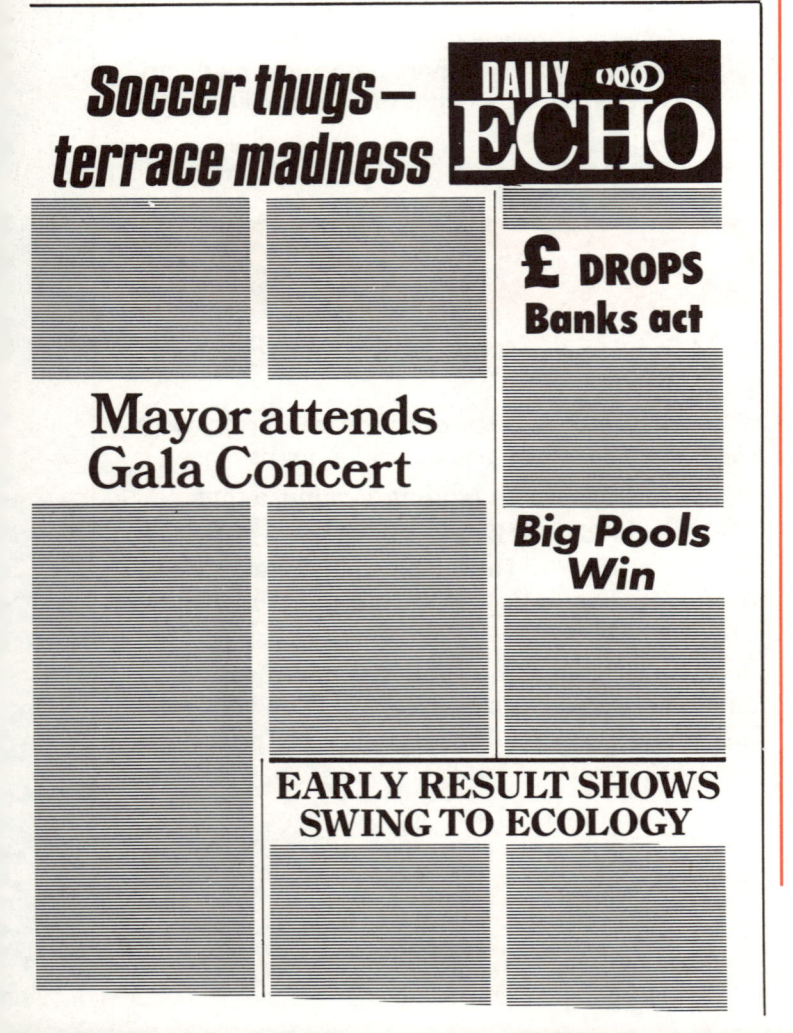

Ease of access

Newspapers are easily found. If you do not have one delivered to your door, you can easily buy one from your local newsagent, or alternatively, you can usually find copies of them at your nearest main library. Libraries normally keep copies of the daily and local newspapers on stands where everybody can read them. We will look more closely at daily or national newspapers, those dealing with items of interest to the whole country, in Unit 36, but in this one we will concentrate on local newspapers.

Bias

Before we go any further, however, it is important to remember that all newspaper owners are in the business to sell as many newspapers as possible and to make money; because of this it is possible that you will find newspaper articles which are biased in one way or another. For example, an editor would not wish to publish an article which would result in his paper being taken to the law courts or that would upset the person, or group of people who were providing the money to keep the paper running. Alternatively he may be tempted to **interpret** the facts in such a way as to cause a sensation and increase sales. It is always useful, therefore, when using newspaper reports to find another source of information to back up or **substantiate** the first article.

35.2 Rich source of local information

Local newspapers can provide you, the historian, with a lot of useful information, especially if you decide to do a local project in Volume 3. Some local papers were established in the 1700s so it is possible to see not only the general way in which your local area has changed, but you can also trace the development of individual features within the county, for example, the county fire brigade or county sports team. All you need is the patience to search for the information you require.

The interesting thing about local newspapers is that it is sometimes possible to find out useful historical facts about your area while searching for something completely different. For instance, imagine that you have chosen to do a local project and you decide to get as much information as you can about your local fire brigade. In this case we will use the example of the Reading Volunteer Fire Brigade in Berkshire. While searching through the old copies of your local newspaper you are certain to find many references to fires this brigade was called out to deal with. It is possible to extract useful **unwitting testimony** about your local area from reading such reports. Look at the following extract. It is a genuine press report of a fire which took place in the centre of Reading in Berkshire in April 1891.

'An alarming fire, one which might have resulted in serious consequences, broke out in Broad Street, Reading, a few minutes before eleven o'clock on Saturday night, in a grocery store at the back of Mr Stevens' shop, between Broad Street and Friar Street. Mr Stevens had recently had additional supplies in, and the fire burned rapidly. Information of the fire was conveyed to the Volunteer Fire Brigade station by a stranger and sixteen men of the brigade with the steam engine and hose-truck were soon on the spot. The police also arrived with the hose-truck and a manual engine. The hose-truck was first set to work at a standpipe opposite Mr Board's and then the volunteer steam engine took its place. The police engine was set to work opposite Mr Martin's tailor shop. The Maiden Erlegh Brigade with their engine arrived later and got to work opposite the post office. A large crowd had gathered, and somewhat interfered with the hose, which, it is stated, was cut. The flames spread to adjoining properties, the premises of the Star Tea Company, Messrs Line & Sons, Messrs Dann, Mr Biddle's stables in Laud Place, Messrs Milwards' workshop, and Mr Archer's oil stores being attacked. Barrels of petroleum were wheeled out from these stores. The horses were removed from Mr Donovan's repository and taken to Early, but fortunately the fire was prevented from getting hold of the stables. Mr Board's (grocers) premises were also saved. For about an hour little appreciable effect was produced upon the flames, but, by degrees, the united efforts of the firemen gained the upper hand, and by between three and four o'clock the fire was got under. A standpipe was left in the charge of some men to watch the fire, which broke out again, but was put out by means of the standpipe. Mr Steven's loss is estimated at £1100 . . .'

35.3 The witting and unwitting testimonies

If you were only interested in the Reading Volunteer Fire Brigade there are many facts in this extract that would be of interest to you. You are told the number of men who attended: sixteen, and how the fire truck was powered; steam. You are told that the police also arrived with their own hose-truck and manual engine (one powered by hand). You can also work out how long it took to get the fire under control; it started a few minutes before eleven o'clock and was 'got under' between three and four o'clock.

More important for general historical interest is that there is plenty of useful information in this extract about the town itself in 1891. Broad Street, the main street in the town, and Friar Street, are still there, but Laud Place no longer exists. Mr Martin's tailor shop has gone and so has the Star Tea Company. The shop on fire, Mr Stevens has gone as well as Mr Biddle's. Mr Archer's shop closed in the 1960s but Mr Milward's shop is still in existence as a thriving shoe shop. It also informs the historian that Laud Place, in the centre of the town had stables, and that 'Barrels of petroleum were brought out from Mr Archer's oil store'. Can you imagine anyone being allowed to keep petrol barrels in a shop in the centre of your town today? What does this tell you about safety standards in 1891?

Fig. 35.2 A modern day picture showing the scene of the fire

All these facts, and there are many more if you look carefully at the extract, have been obtained while researching for a different topic altogether. We will now look more closely at how you can find newspapers which will give you this type of information and how it can be used.

Unit 35 continued

35.4 Where to find old newspapers

When you have finished with your newspaper at home you probably throw it away, but most main libraries buy copies of all the local, and some national, papers and keep them on file for reference. After a period of time many of them are sent to the local records' office where they can be found and used by historians. Occasionally you will find these old copies kept on shelves in large newspaper-sized binders, but because these can take up a lot of valuable space some records' offices store material such as this on **micro-film**. The newspaper pages are photographed and kept on a roll of film slightly larger than the one you may put in your camera. These rolls are kept in their own labelled box. Many more newspapers can be kept in this way because these boxes take up little space.

35.5 How to look at them

If you wish to look at a particular, newspaper you find the film with the correct label, for example, '*The Observer* 1891' and ask the assistant to put it in a special machine which displays the page on to a small screen in front of you. You wind on, or move, the film until the page you require appears on the screen and then you can read it. (Some rolls of film contain more than one year's newspapers so you may have to wind for some time before the page you require appears.) Some micro-film machines are kept in darkened rooms, and because there is a bright light shining through the film to allow you to read the writing on it, you may find it is a strain on your eyes, therefore, when you start to use micro-film read it only for a short period of time, have a break, and go back to it. Micro-film is very easy to read and it saves you having to turn over many very delicate newspaper pages. Usually you will know the date of the actual paper you require, for example, 4 April 1891, but you may not know the page on which the information you require appears. In this case the only thing to do is to read quickly, or **scan**, the newspaper. You do not need to read every article, just look at the headlines until you see one that may be relevant.

35.6 Using the indexes

The old newspapers you require from the records' office can be found using the same routine as in Unit 23. You are likely to find a reference to the material by looking it up in the subject index, in our example, 'The Reading Volunteer Fire Brigade', or perhaps 'Fire'. You may wish to look up a certain incident when the fire brigade was called out to a specific area, in which case you may find a reference to it in the parish index. Write down the reference number, complete the document requisition form and hand it in at the desk and wait. (To refresh your memory re-read Unit 23.)

35.7 New leads

We have seen that when you have found the newspaper report you want, you can sometimes gain a lot more information about your local area than you had expected. A report can also often provide you with the starting point for further study. Having found the information about the fire in Reading in 35.2 it would be worthwhile finding a detailed map of this area of the town in 1891 and comparing it with one as near to the present day as possible. It would be interesting to see if the shops are still there today or if they are owned by the same family, or if they have changed you can find out what they are used for today.

The official report

Fires were not only reported by the press, they were described by the fire brigade themselves and kept on file as an official account. It would be possible, therefore, to support the press report by finding the fire officer's report and comparing

Fig. 35.1 Diagram illustrating newspaper microstorage

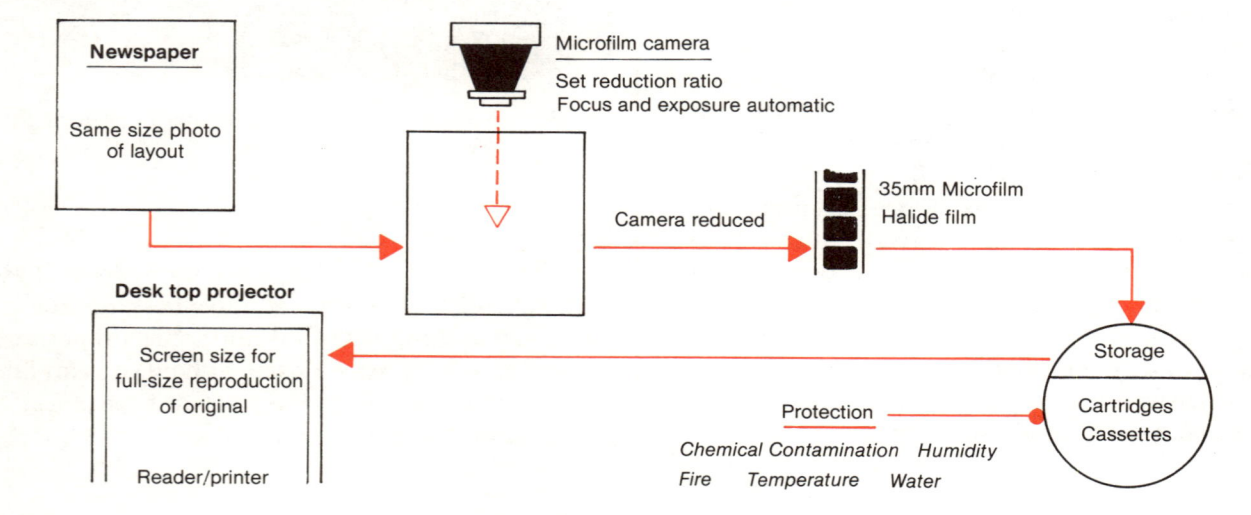

them. These official reports also provide you with more detailed information. The reports should also be available at your records' office or in this case you may find that the fire brigade keeps them on their own files, in which case you would have to write to your local fire station and ask for permission to see them. The following example is taken from the official report on the fire damage at the fire described in Unit 35.2

'**Star Tea Company**, 32 Broad Street. Shop 90ft by 20ft and contents severely damaged by fire, heat, smoke, water and breakage; part of roof off. Cellar under and contents damaged by water. Rest of house slightly by smoke. Insurance, Hand-in-Hand.

Messrs Line and Sons 30 Broad Street. 20ft by 6ft, roof damaged by fire, and contents under by water. Insurance, Lancashire.

Messrs Milward, 34 Broad Street. Roof of workshop slightly damaged by breakage; contents by water. Insurance unknown.'

The report goes on to list all the buildings damaged in the fire. This report provides the reader with some useful information. We now have the actual addresses and size of the buildings, the damage caused by the fire and water, and surprisingly the names of the insurance companies who would have had to pay out for all the repairs. There are more facts here than you would probably need for a simple project, but they give you an idea of how much can be obtained from a press report. There are new starting points even in this official report; for instance, you could find out if the insurance companies mentioned still exist today.

35.8 Further study

We have only looked at one specific example of historical material available from a local newspaper. There are many more topics you could research. If you are interested in sport you could find out about your local football team or county cricket or netball team. In modern papers there is usually a number of pages dealing only with sport, but in older papers you may find that this information is mixed up with all the other news, so you may have to search through more pages. Whatever local topic you may choose to do in Volume 3, if it requires the use of newspapers, the routine is always the same. Remember, as you are reading the material for your topic, to look out for other facts that may be of general interest and give you some background information for the area you are studying.

Activities

We have said that your local newspaper will be useful to you if you decide to do a local project in Volume 3. You may find that some local newspapers in your area are no longer published or they have joined (**amalgamated**) with another newspaper and possibly changed their names. Go to your local library and find out **all** the names of the local papers which have printed the news about your area from the earliest possible date (few were published before 1750). If a paper is no longer printed try to find out the years during which it was. Make a list of all these papers and their dates so that you have a reference. Then if you wish to look up the facts of a particular event at a particular time you will know the newspapers available at the time and, therefore, those likely to contain the information.

Summary

1 Newspapers are cheap sources of historical information.

2 Local newspapers are very useful if you are researching an historical topic dealing with your local area.

3 While researching this topic you may find additional facts about the general history of your local area.

4 Newspaper articles can be biased, so it is always useful to use another source of information to make sure the details contained in the article are correct.

5 Many old copies of local newspapers are kept either at main libraries or at the county records' office.

6 Local newspapers are very useful to the historian studying a local topic.

7 In order to find out the specific newspaper you require at the records' office, use the same routine as that described in Unit 23.

8 Many old newspapers are photographed and stored on micro-film.

9 Micro-film is very easy to use, but when you start, read only for a short period of time.

10 Newspaper reports are very useful for providing you with a starting point for further investigation.

Revision

Local newspapers

Below you will see an example similar to the one in Unit 35. It is a press report from *The Observer* newspaper dated 11 February 1893, and it concerns a fire which occurred in the Caversham area of Reading on that date. Read the extract carefully and then answer the questions following it. They are the type of questions you should ask yourself when looking at any material of this kind.

'A fire, which resulted in the total destruction of the tap in connection with the White Hart Hotel, Caversham, broke out on Monday afternoon shortly after two o'clock. The building was a low one, and was situated on the south side of the hotel itself and was detached. The first intimation of the conflagration was given by Inspector May, of the G.W.R. who noticed smoke issuing from the roof near one of the chimneys. He at once apprised the inmates and lost no time in telephoning from the adjacent hotel to the Reading Volunteer Fire Brigade and the Police Station.

In the meantime as much as possible was done in the direction of saving the portable property. A hand hose was affixed to the supply pipe, but was of little avail. Shortly after the call the Chief Engineer of the Volunteer Fire Brigade, Palmer, arrived with Mr Rawstorne, a member of the brigade, and a stand-pipe was fixed. A few minutes later a contingent of police arrived on the spot, being quickly followed by the steam fire engine. The gates leading down to the river on the East side of Caversham Road having been burst open, the engine was stationed close to the river, whence, of course, an illimitable supply of water was obtained. The hose was run out and in a short time several powerful jets of water were being thrown on the burning building.

By this time the flames had fairly got the mastery of the place, which, being old and the contents – spirits and so on – being inflammable, burned fiercely. At one time there was a likelihood of the hotel itself becoming ignited, but fortunately, owing to the efforts of the firemen, all the danger was averted about 3.30. The roof fell in and the premises were completely gutted.

It was necessary to bring the hose-pipes across the road, and consequently traffic was for a time stopped. A large crowd of persons witnessed the conflagration, but the police kept them from impeding the operations of the brigades. The Maiden Erlegh Fire Brigade had also been summoned by telephone, and responded to the call with alacrity, being on the spot about 3.30. Their services, however, were not then required. The origin of the fire is supposed to have been a defective flue. The building was in the occupation of Mr A.G. Bona, landlord of the White Hart; it belonged to the Corporation of Reading, and the loss, we believe, is covered by insurance. The contents of the premises were insured in the London and Lancashire office. The damage is officially stated to be as follows:

Bar, about 20ft by 9ft and three rooms on the ground floor and contents burned out, and roof off. Four rooms in basement and contents severely damaged by fire, heat, smoke and water . . .'

1 The word 'tap' appears in line 2. What do you think it refers to?
2 Where did the fire take place?
3 Using the facts available, describe the building.
4 What does the word **'conflagration'** mean?
5 Who first reported the fire, and for which company did he work?
6 What did he do first?
7 Whom did he telephone?
8 What is 'portable property' in lines 15–16 of the extract?
9 What was the name of the Chief Engineer of the Volunteer Brigade?
10 Who arrived with him?
11 What was their first action?
12 What followed the contingent of police to the scene?
13 Where did the fire engine get its supply of water?
14 How did the engine get to this spot?
15 Why did the building burn quickly?
16 At what time was the hotel saved from the fire?
17 Which fire brigade arrived, but was not required?
18 What does the word **'alacrity'** mean in line 47?
19 What was considered to be the cause of the fire?
20 Who owned the building?
21 Who was living in the building at the time of the fire?
22 Who had insured the contents of the building?
23 Describe the damage to the building.
24 What four things caused the damage?
25 Having read the report your next step in the investigation of this fire may be to go and see if the hotel still exists. But what else would you have to do to check that the facts in this report are genuine?

Having collected this information, check the answers at the back of the book and use them to describe the fire **in your own words**. Do not look at the original passage until you have completed the task. Then compare them. How different are they – they should be very similar.

Unit 36

National newspapers

36.1 Outlook of national papers

National newspapers contain different news and stories from local ones and need to be used in a different way. They are written in such a way as to interest the whole country, so the information they contain is of a more general interest.

Different styles of paper

They are also often more **biased** than local papers. Some support a particular political party or the views of a certain group of people, so the writing contained in the paper may well be biased towards the group. You will soon realize if there is any bias in the way the articles are written in individual newspapers. Some will always praise the actions of a certain political party whether or not they are in power at the time. All national newspapers are different and cater for varied tastes.

Some have more photographs than others, some contain cartoons and games and some have more sports pages or financial (money) pages than others. Therefore, if you require a national newspaper to provide you with information for a particular topic, you need to find the one which will give you the facts as accurately as possible, and which does not **sensationalize** the news.

National newspapers in Britain during peacetime report the facts from home and abroad with few **restrictions**. The information is available immediately and is reasonably accurate. However, if you need to look at a newspaper printed in the war years, especially 1939 to 1945, you need to be very careful and selective in your choice.

36.2 Restrictions during wartime

The press had a great responsibility during wartime. We have said that newspapers are easily obtainable and provide you with immediate facts and, of course, they can be read by anyone, including, in war-years, secret agents working for an enemy power. So if all the details of bombing raids, or lack of food, or the sinking of a merchant ship were printed in the newspaper, the information could get back to the enemy and could be used for **propaganda** purposes. It was because of this that the news of which towns or cities had been bombed was not printed until two days after the raid had taken place. Only the names of those factories which **had not** been damaged were allowed to appear in the paper.

The newspapers were also responsible for 'keeping up the spirits of the people' at home. If the population on 'The Home Front' read about setbacks or defeats their **morale** might have declined and their desire to continue with the war effort might have been affected. This led to **distorted** headlines which occasionally turned great allied defeats into 'minor setbacks' or in some cases victories. For example, the disastrous attempt to raid the coast of France at Dieppe, when many soldiers, mostly Canadians, were killed while trying to climb the cliffs, was reported in two British newspapers at the time under the headlines:

> **BIG HUN LOSSES in nine hour DIEPPE battle**

> **Dieppe: HOW WE STORMED HITLER'S STRONGHOLD**

Little was said about the appalling losses, and so if you read this report you would see a very biased and one-sided opinion of what happened. This is an excellent example of a situation where you need to look at another source, in this case, perhaps, the official history of the battle, in order to find out the truth.

36.3 Tracing a particular newspaper

If you wish to use a newspaper printed on a certain day you may find a copy at your local library or records' office, but if not, you can always contact the newspaper office. (Some newspapers have been taken over by others so if you cannot find the one you require, you may need to find out its new owners or the paper it has been joined with.) The main centre of the press in England is Fleet Street in London, but some newspapers have a northern office in Manchester, so if you need to look at **back-copies** you may have to visit the centre nearest to you.

Before you go, ask yourself whether the amount

of information you are likely to find will be worth the journey, because if you have to travel a long way it may be simpler and less time-consuming to try to find it elsewhere. If you do decide to go always telephone the newspaper office first to check if they have an example of the article you need, and whether or not they will allow you to make a copy.

Newspapers turn up everywhere!

Even if you do not want any specific information from them, old newspapers can be very interesting to read and sometimes you do not need to travel very far to find them. Sometimes they were used to insulate walls and to cut out draughts in old houses, and sometimes they were spread out on shelves in a shed or greenhouse, and occasionally you may find that newspaper was spread over the floor before the carpet was laid on top. The important thing to remember is that all newspapers have a date on them and so it is easy to give a date to the events and articles in that particular copy. It is also possible to buy a national newspaper for the day you were born. You could find out what was happening in the world on your birthday and possibly use some of the information on your personal time-line in Unit 2.

36.4 Tracing history through advertisements

One fascinating part of old newspapers is not necessarily the articles they contain, but the advertisements. They show what people were interested in buying at the time the newspaper was printed. The date on the paper can give you the exact date when certain clothes were in fashion or a particular washing powder was popular or a certain cure was available for the treatment of various illnesses.

It is possible to do a very interesting project on newspaper advertisements of the past because they can provide the reader with an idea of the **social history** of the time i.e. the everyday objects and events which affected people's lives. It is also possible to compare advertisements of products in the 1930s, or even earlier, with advertisements for the same product today. You can see how the article itself may have changed and also the way in which the 'selling' of the product has changed i.e. how the drawings or catch-phrases differ today from past examples.

Newspapers, both local and national, can be useful to an historian. You are more likely to use local newspapers than national ones because you will probably find them more useful for your study and easier to obtain, but remember, whichever example you use, you must try to check the facts in any newspaper report with another source before you can believe its accuracy and use them in a project or essay.

Activities

Try to find advertisements from the past for goods still available today and make a note of the differences between how they were 'sold' to the public then and now.

You can include goods such as breakfast cereals, soaps, washing powder, medicines etc.

Summary

1 Remember again that newspaper reports are only one person's point of view.

2 Newspaper coverage of the news in wartime was often distorted so as not to lower the morale of the people.

3 The date on the newspaper can give you an immediate aid to dating the information contained in the articles and advertisements.

4 Advertisements can be a useful source of historical information about the house and homes of the past. They show the sort of articles people were prepared to buy and have in their homes.

5 Whenever possible, check the accuracy of the facts from newspaper articles with other sources.

Unit 37

Museums

In Unit 29 we looked at ways in which artefacts can be a useful aid in helping an historian decide what life may have been like in the past. Some of these articles are on show in country houses open to the public, some can be seen on archaeological digs, but most are displayed in museums. There are many different types of museum, too many to describe in detail, but they can be broadly divided into three categories: local museums, specialist museums, and open-air/live museums.

37.1 Local museums

Most local, or general museums cover all aspects of history in the area in which it is situated. They usually display articles which illustrate life in the past in as many areas of local life as possible, including housing and household goods, agriculture, education and occasionally the articles relating to an important local industry.

Most of the exhibits in this type of museum are kept in glass cabinets and each one is described in as much detail as space will allow. Unfortunately, because these museums cover such a wide range of interests, space is usually very limited, so many of the artefacts are not on display, but kept 'behind the scenes' in storage. Therefore, if you visit a museum and cannot see the example of the article you wish to look at, it is often worth asking the **curator** if there is one in store which you may examine.

Usually the staff will be very helpful if they know that you have a genuine interest, so before you put them to a lot of trouble, make sure you know exactly what you are looking for. Alternatively your area may have a schools' museum service which lends articles to schools for closer examination in the classroom. If you have a particular interest you may like to ask your teacher to write to the service and request articles which may help you in your study.

Fig. 37.1 Development of the tractor (Museum of English Rural Life, Reading)

Fig. 37.2 Visiting a rural museum can give you an idea of how people farmed many years ago

37.2 Specialist museums

In some areas of the country you will find specialist museums. These specialize in only one topic or subject, for example, the history of a local industry, and they collect and display as many articles and as much documentary evidence as possible about the subject they are concerned with. Again, because of lack of space, many examples are kept in storage.

These museums occasionally put on **special exhibitions** dealing with one particular aspect of their subject. For instance, the Science Museum in London which contains articles dealing with all branches of science including domestic science, sometimes has special displays on, for example, manned-flight or the history of space travel. (It is worth looking out for these 'specials' because they may deal with the exact topic you are interested in.)

Getting around the exhibits

Museums such as the Science, the Natural History and the British Museum in London are very large and you could easily take a complete day exploring one of them. They are interesting places just to browse around, but it is very easy to miss important exhibits. To help you as much as possible in your visit, some museums such as the Imperial War Museum, also in London, will provide you with a worksheet which will guide you through most of the important features on display. These sheets are usually available at the bookshop. (If you decide beforehand that you will use a worksheet, remember to take a piece of cardboard or a clip-board with you to rest your work on.)

Examples of specialist museums

There are many specialist museums, again too many to describe in detail, but a few examples are: the Cricket Museum at Lord's Cricket Ground in London, the National Railway Museum in York, the National Motor Museum at Beaulieu in Hampshire and the Costume Museum in Bath. If you wish to visit a museum it is possible to find all the information you require about it such as times of opening and admission charges, if any, from a **museum guide** in the reference section of a library. It should also list the specialist ones under their subject headings.

Unit 37 continued

37.3 Open-air or live museums

In recent years there has been a move away from museums with static artefacts in glass cases, to those where the articles, often too large to fit into any museum building, are kept in their original condition. These open-air museums contain not only artefacts, but complete houses and shops and even small factories. If the museum staff find a good example of an old building which is scheduled to be demolished, they will offer to buy it, take it down brick by brick, and rebuild it on the museum site. In some cases these buildings come alive again; if it is a Victorian butcher's shop it may sell meat, or if it is a public house it may sell drinks. Everything in the building would be as authentic as possible, and if you visit a museum 'community' such as this, you would be stepping back into the past. Some keen enthusiasts actually dress up in the correct costume and take on the role of butcher or householder or carpenter, and bring the museum to life.

Steam railways

Another example of live museums, which in some cases have become thriving businesses, are steam railways. In some areas of the country a group of interested people have got together and bought a section of railway track, including stations, engines and rolling stock, and recreated a steam railway of the past. Again all the articles are genuine and not only can you see them in their original setting, but you can also ride on the trains.

Some of the railways have become more than museums, they provide a regular train service between stations and have therefore attracted many 'commuters'. Others have been used as film-sets to provide the scenery for any film needing the use of a station or steam locomotive.

37.3 Getting the most out of your visit

With any museum, from the small local one to the large specialist or open-air one, the main thing to remember is that you must be observant. They are all interesting to visit, but if you have a particular study in mind it is worth asking yourself a series of questions to help structure your trip. If possible you can make more than one visit; after the first one you will know what the museum contains, and so on the second visit you will be able to concentrate more fully on the section which interests you most. However, always be prepared to spend a long time browsing because if you are a keen historian you will find that it is always difficult dragging yourself away from an interesting museum.

Activities

Using either a good local atlas or books from your library, make a list of all the museums and historic houses in your local area which may be useful to visit before starting your local project in Volume 3.

Summary

1 There are three broad categories of museum.

(a) Local museums: those which deal entirely with all aspects of community life in the local area.

(b) Specialist museums: those concentrating on all matters concerned with one particular subject area.

(c) Open-air museums: containing larger artefacts including buildings and which recreate working and living conditions of the past, including transport, (steam preservation societies.)

2 Remember, only a certain number of artefacts can be displayed in a museum at any one time. The article you may wish to examine could be in storage.

3 **Always be observant.** Take a notebook with you to record the things you see. A camera would always be useful at an open-air museum. (But remember to write down the exact subject of the photograph in case you forget before the film is developed.)

4 If you are studying artefacts for a specific study, ask yourself questions about it to concentrate your thoughts on the subject. How big? What was it used for? What is it made of?

Unit 38
Sources

The following diagrams show the main sources, primary and secondary and other information. They are a summary of those we have looked at in this book and we will investigate in Volumes 2 and 3. There are spaces available for you to add extra sources which you find during your own studies.

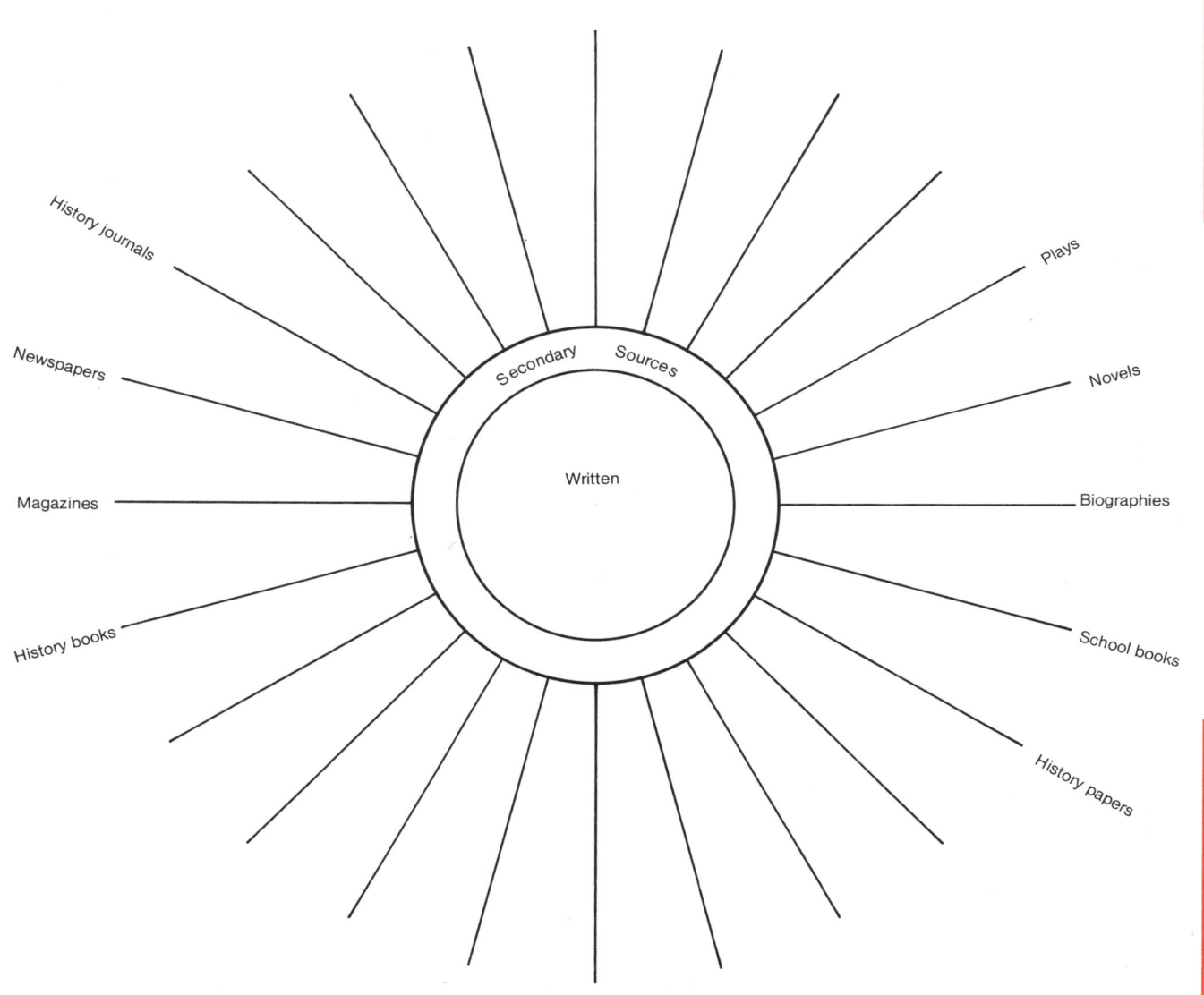

Written — Secondary Sources

- History journals
- Newspapers
- Magazines
- History books
- Plays
- Novels
- Biographies
- School books
- History papers

Fig. 38.1

Unit 38 continued

Fig. 38.2

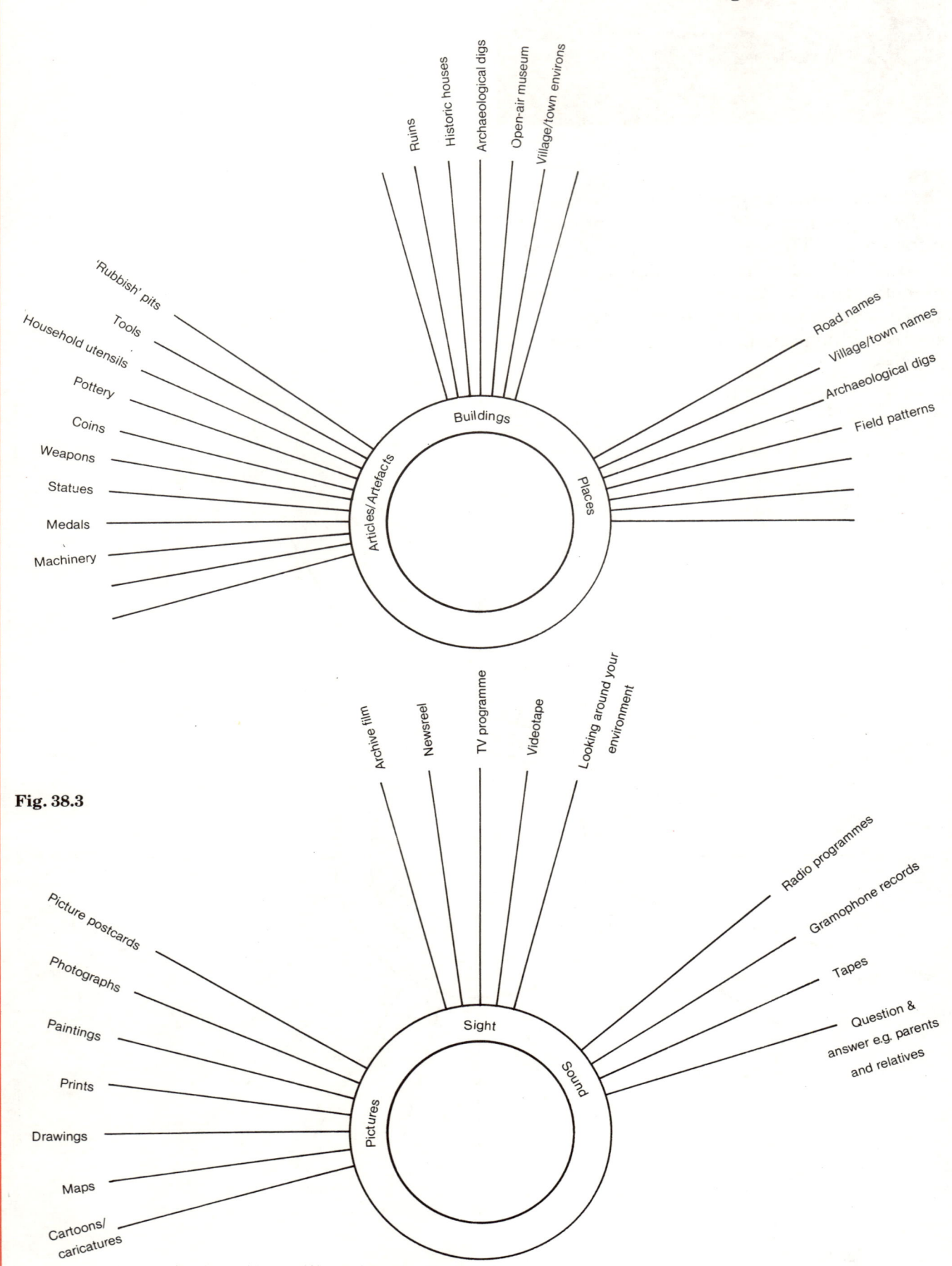

Places (Buildings / Articles/Artefacts):
- Ruins
- Historic houses
- Archaeological digs
- Open-air museum
- Village/town environs
- Road names
- Village/town names
- Archaeological digs
- Field patterns
- 'Rubbish' pits
- Tools
- Household utensils
- Pottery
- Coins
- Weapons
- Statues
- Medals
- Machinery

Fig. 38.3

Sight / Sound (Pictures):
- Archive film
- Newsreel
- TV programme
- Videotape
- Looking around your environment
- Radio programmes
- Gramophone records
- Tapes
- Question & answer e.g. parents and relatives
- Picture postcards
- Photographs
- Paintings
- Prints
- Drawings
- Maps
- Cartoons/caricatures

123

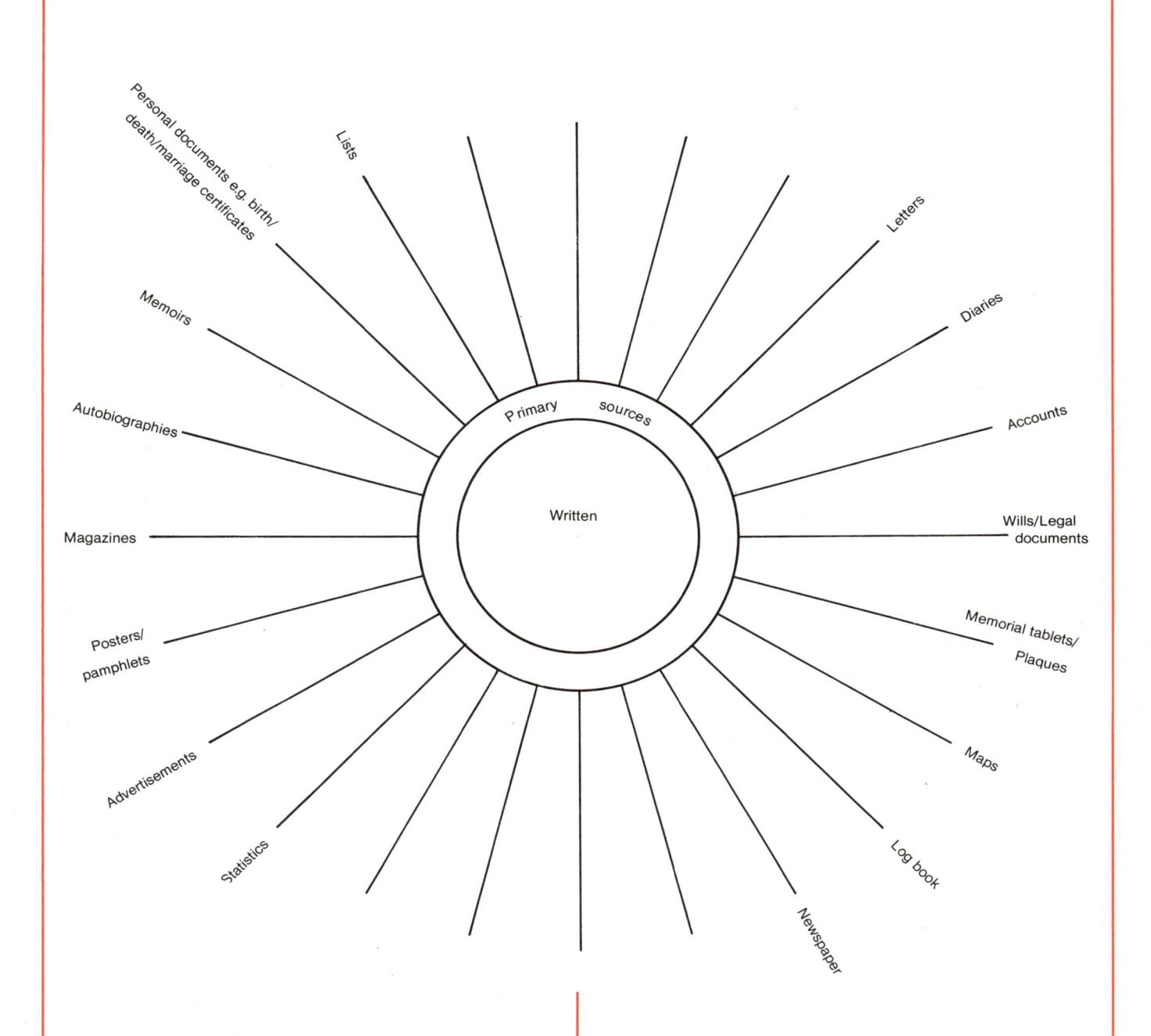

Primary sources

Written

- Personal documents e.g. birth/death/marriage certificates
- Lists
- Letters
- Diaries
- Accounts
- Wills/Legal documents
- Memorial tablets/Plaques
- Maps
- Log book
- Newspaper
- Statistics
- Advertisements
- Posters/pamphlets
- Magazines
- Autobiographies
- Memoirs

Fig. 38.4

Activities

Draw two diagrams as above and label one Family project and the other Local project. Draw lines out from the circle and mark on the sources which will be useful to you when investigating these projects in Volume 3.

Answers

Unit 1

Text page 10: Manchester United
Paul McCartney

1. Now
2. Environment
3. Dictionary
4. James Smith
5. 7.10 a.m.
6. Cereal, toast, coffee

More activities

(a) Charles Letts & Co Ltd
(b) Martin L. Parsons
(c) Bachelor of Arts
(d) 1986

Unit 2

Text page 13: you could simply ask someone else who was there

Unit 3

1. Jayne Torvill and Christopher Dean
2. Nigel Lawson
3. Duke of Gloucester – 10 June
4. Argentina
5. Marriage of Prince Charles to Lady Diana Spencer
6. Argentina – Falkland Islands
7. 1974
8. New Zealand
9. Rt. Hon. Edward Heath
10. Los Angeles

Unit 5

1. 10
2. Labour
3. £1.30
4. Labour – because Clement Attlee, the leader of the Labour Party was PM from 1945 to 1951
5. September 1968
6. Does not include – lorries, motor cycles or other forms of motorized transport
7. £1.90
8. £4.50
9. 15 February 1971
10. Sir Alec Douglas-Home
11. Ramsay MacDonald, Stanley Baldwin, Winston Churchill, Harold Wilson
12. 1979
13. 2 years 11 months (3 years minus 14 days)
14. 7 387 075
15. 5 299 925 (12 687 000 – 7 387 075)

Unit 5 More Activities

(a) £2.80
(b) 7 387 075
(c) 1940
(d) Winston Churchill
(e) Three: Sir Anthony Eden, Sir Winston Churchill, Sir Alex Douglas-Home
(f) £5 (1969)
(g) 13½p
(h) £4.50 – 40p = £4.10
(i) 1924 £1.40 – Labour
1978 £49.40 – Labour
a rise of £48
(j) 9 days, 12.90

Unit 6

Text page 24: (a) Decade (b) Century (c) Millenium

1. (a) 18th (f) 9th
   (b) 19th (g) 17th
   (c) 8th (h) 16th
   (d) 5th (i) 10th
   (e) 20th (j) 14th

2. (a) 46
   (b) 310
   (c) 100
   (d) 95
   (e) 848

Unit 7

Text page 26: Fig. 7.1: Queen Elizabeth II
Fig. 7.2: Queen Elizabeth I

1. (a) Queen Elizabeth II
   (b) 1952
   (c) State occasions, opening new buildings, meetings of foreign heads of state
2. (a) Queen Elizabeth I
   (b) 1558 to 1603
   (c) 16th and 17th
3. (a) Oil
   (b) Soldering iron
   (c) Aprons, mop caps
   (d) To protect their clothes and hair
   (e) In the 1920s

Unit 8

(a) Guido Fawkes
(b) Protestant
(c) Flanders
(d) King Phillip III
(e) Catholic: Fawkes was converted to the Catholic faith before joining the Spanish Army. King Phillip was the King of Spain and therefore the head of the army. Catholics in England sent Fawkes to King Phillip to persuade him to invade England. They would not have done this if Phillip had been a Protestant.
(f) John Johnson
(g) 11.00 p.m.
(h) The Tower of London
(i) Four days
(j) James I

Unit 9

1. In 1597 the wages of both skilled and unskilled workers was far below the price of a 1kg bag of wheat. Therefore they went hungry. In 1682 however the wages were higher than the price of wheat and so could be bought by the skilled worker, but not necessarily the unskilled.
2. In some areas, road sweeper, newspaperseller, flower-seller. Also crow-scarers in rural areas.
3. *The Water-Babies*

Revision word search
1 Plantagenet
2 Lancastrian
3 Spain
4 Saxon
5 Marston Moor
6 Tudor
7 Angevin
8 Regency
9 Victorian
10 Flanders
11 Parliament
12 Norman
13 Stuart
14 Georgian
15 Guy
16 Decade
17 Rupert
18 Samuel Pepys
19 Tinker
20 Civil
21 Anglo
22 King
23 Century
24 Millenium
25 Ages
26 Parent
27 Now
28 Patience
29 Wilson
30 Thorpe
31 Bronze
32 BC
33 Anno
34 Guido
35 Home

Unit 10
(a) Danes
(b) 877
(c) Swanage Bay
(d) Edgar 'Taffy' Evans
(e) Capt Robert Falcon Scott
(f) Antarctic – South Pole
(g) Taffy
(h) 18 January 1912
(i) They died
(j) 800 miles

1 12
2 33
3 256
4 1824
5 629
6 XLII
7 CCLXV
8 MDCCCL
9 DCXLIV
10 CXI

Unit 11
1 1642
2 King Charles I
3 Prince Rupert
4 It was seized by the Parliamentary Army
5 Sir Edward Verney
6 James I
7 France and Spain
8 Eleven Years Tyranny
9 Arrest five members of Parliament
10 Nottingham
11 Edgehill
12 Yes, King Charles features in both; Example C explains the events before the Civil War. Example A describes the Battle of Edgehill, the first battle in the Civil War
13 Sir John Smith
14 Wooten-Wawen in Warwickshire
15 He retrieved the Royal Standard from the Parliamentary Army
16 Bramdean
17 Andover, 30 March 1944
18 28
19 Nephew
20 Yes, both have something to do with the Battle of Edgehill. Example A describes it and Example D explains that Sir John Smith fought at the Battle of Edgehill and retrieved the King's Standard there. For this act of heroism he was knighted.
21 Yes, because C explains the events leading to Civil War and the Battle of Edgehill and John Smith fought in the Battle of Edgehill
22 1770s
23 Chemise
24 Hair was brushed back from the forehead and ringlets at the back were tied up with a small ribbon
25 No
26 Portsmouth, Dover
27 Plymouth
28 Wealthy and noble settlers, both Roman Catholics and Anglicans
29 Not directly. The only link is that two of the places Salem (1630) and Providence (1636) were established during the Eleven Years Tyranny, mentioned in Example C. But this is a very loose link. Example E has nothing to do with these items dealing with the civil war.

Revision units 1 – 12 Treasure trail
Sequence should be:
1, 5, 8, 2, 11, 6, 14, 13, 9, 3, 12, 10, 7, 4

Unit 13
1 George Burt – gilt fish weather vane from Billingsgate fish market, facade of the Mercers Hall, Wellington Clock Tower
2 Picture of a bollard on a London street corner
3 A gun-emplacement or 'Pill-Box'

Unit 14
2 The aeroplane developed quickly especially during the years 1914 to 1918 and 1939 to 1945 because it became a very important piece of equipment in 20th-century warfare. The designers, therefore, had to design and build faster and more efficient 'fighters and bombers'. Much of their work was used later to develop passenger aircraft

Unit 15
1 Because the British were his enemies
2 Official war histories or a neutral observer's account
3
Primary	Secondary
Maps	History books
Autobiographies	Hollywood movie
Documents	History journal
Carved inscriptions	Biographies
Church/parish registers	Videotapes
Letters	School text books

Unit 16
1 Four
2 False
3 Overalls and mop caps
4 To stop their hair being caught in the machinery
5 Arm power
6 Fan belt as a central spindle
7 Gas
8 Twenty-five
9 No – cold

Revision units 16 – 17 Practice with photographs
1 (a) The founder of the Methodist Church
   (b) 1774
   (c) The German Luftwaffe
2 (a) A medical room
   (b) Nurse – the uniform
   (c) Gas
   (d) Medicines

(e) The costume worn by the ladies with the nurse
  (f) Very sparse – no bed or couch, few examples of medicines
  (g) Very bare
3 (a) Four
  (b) Hat, jacket and trousers
  (c) Brick/stone
  (d) The cart is taking stone from the quarries to the quay for transportation by boat to the larger boats and then to London
  (e) The stone was taken to London and the street bollards were brought back as ballast in the boats
  (f) Witting testimony – the photographer intended to show the transportation of coal
4 (a) False – cameras were not invented in 1810
  (b) Putting stone into boats
  (c) Lifting stone from the quarry to the boats
  (d) Costume, fashions, equipment, boats, surrounding areas
  (e) The large, older man in the centre of the picture
5 **General**
(a) What does the photographer want me to see in this picture? What else can I see that may be useful to me as an historian?
(b) Where was the photographer standing when he took this picture *or* in which year was this photograph taken?
(c) The troops were coming towards the camera so the photographer could only have stood in the middle of the battlefield. Secondly, in the picture of the gas-attack the men are too clean.
(d) Spreading information either false or true for some purpose

The shutter speeds were so slow that if anyone moved they would appear as a blur in the photograph
(e) Libraries, museums, personal photograph albums, newspaper collections

Unit 18

1 6.30 a.m.
2 Very wet and windy to start with but sunny later
3 Golf and cricket
4 Bad roadworks on M4 caused traffic-jams
5 No – because he knows what the traffic is usually like – there is no mention of a train at all
6 Miss Simms; the finance meeting
7 Wee Waif – interesting people, food good, but expensive
8 No
9 Coffee machine, M4, cricket on television
Text page 59: not entirely; the driver is putting all the blame on the other person

Unit 19

1 (a) Fenner
  (b) Tom
  (c) Cow's tongue
  (d) The servants did not have time to prepare a hot meal
  (e) With powder; head lice
  (f) 13¾ years
  (g) Larks
  (h) The butcher and the weaver
  (i) So that they could go unrecognized
  (j) In Moorfields
  (k) The King's Theatre
  (l) 'the most insipid, ridiculous play that ever I saw in my life!'
  (m) The state of the weather
  (n) 1.00 a.m.
  (o) He was wealthy, ate well, had servants, was critical of the theatre, went to bed late, very observant
2 (a) Horses were the main method of transport for the wealthy, therefore, someone was needed to make saddles and mend the leather harness
  (b) Plague
  (c) A boat; he mentions his waterman who carried him daily
  (d) They had been coated with pitch to preserve the timber
  (e) Precious metals e.g. gold and silver plates and goblets as ornaments
  (f) Sir Christopher Wren
  (g) It gives a great description of events in London between 1660 and 1669 by someone who was actually there

More activities
John Evelyn

Unit 21

(a) 1932 to 1936
(b) Apart from the sports field, the office workers rarely mixed with the factory workers, and to be a factory girl was considered to be the lowest one could get
(c) By train, walking or bicycling
(d) No collars; the general description of their dress
(e) 'to hide the absence of a collar'
(f) Biscuits and cakes: smell of the ovens, flour and the baking
(g) He uses the words 'by your previous writer' (line 4)
(h) Greasy white coats and long white aprons
(i) They provided power to the machines
(j) Bored
(k) He says that 'I have no cosy memories of that experience' (1st paragraph) and at the end, 'I did not shed a single tear'
(l) He says 'I was not born in your town'
(m) The first writer must have enjoyed working at the factory and had fond memories of it
(n) Trams, overhead belts, closing of factory gates, ancient black machines, 'Familiar songs of the Thirties', the fact that as we find out at the end, the factory is no longer there

Unit 22

Text page 72:
(a) **Boarders** – therefore, a boarding school

1 1949
2 Acting Postal Inspector, the Postal service
3 Christopher J. Morgan
4 Curate
5 England
6 The entry number (128) in the register and also the date
7 Short and long certificates. The short certificate gives only the name and sex of the child and the date and area of registration. The long certificate gives this information plus the place of birth, the names of the parents, and the occupation of the father.
8 1837
9 The Registrar General
10 The Aldwych, St Catherine's House

Unit 23

Aldworth, Alnmouth, Ashford, Bexhill, Bishop Auckland, Bishop Castle, Enfield, Falkirk, Falkland, Hampton, Kingston, Kingswood, Milford, Newmarket, Oxford, Portsmouth, Saltash, Wallingford, Yattendon, Zetland

Unit 24

1 (a) **Celtic** YSTRAD TREFNANT
   Roman LEICESTER DORCHESTER
   Saxon CASTLETON BAMBURGH DALTON
         RAYLEIGH SHEPTON ROMPTON BILSTON
         BARHAM BINGLEY SANDWICK NORTHWICH
         EDINBURGH NEWTON WATLINGTON
         NEWBURGH
   Danish/Viking ATTLEBOROUGH ASHFORDBY
         ALTHORPE SCARBOROUGH
   Others ABBEYTOWN BRIDGENORTH
         AVONMOUTH PORTLAND KENTFORD
         CAMELFORD STOCKBRIDGE HATFIELD
         RINGWOOD
   (b) CASTLETON = Castle Farm;
       BRIDGENORTH = The Northern Bridge to distinguish it from other bridges;
       AVONMOUTH = Settlement at mouth of R Avon;
       SHEPTON = Sheeptown; RAMPTON = Ram farm;
       ATTLEBOROUGH = Fort at Attle;
       BARHAM = Meadow belonging to Bar;
       KENTFORD = Ford or crossing over R Kent;
       CAMELFORD = Ford or crossing over R Camel;
       STOCKBRIDGE = Bridge over rivers used by farm animals (stock); NORTHWICH = North Farm;
       EDINBURGH = Edwin's Fort; NEWTON = New Farm
2 There must have been other forts in the area as this was the middle one
3 Edinburgh is a Saxon settlement and Scarborough was Viking

Revision Units 25 to 28

1 (a) False – After 1500 cannons could destroy castle walls therefore they were not worth building
   (b) True
   (c) True
   (d) True
   (e) True
   (f) True
   (g) False – tiled roof
   (h) False – the oldest building in a village is usually the church
   (i) True
   (j) True
2 Fig. R1 – Modern – not Tudor
   Fig. R2 – Modern
   Fig. R3 – Tudor
   Fig. R4 – Late 19th century

Unit 29

Dates: (a) Between 1741 and 1825 approx 1800
       (b) Between 1576 and 1741 approx 1700
       (c) Between 1825 and 1914 approx 1890
       (d) Between 1914 and 1952 approx 1945
       (e) Between 950 and 1080 approx 1025
       (f) Between 1080 and 1576 approx 1476
       (g) Between 1576 and 1741 approx 1700
       (h) Between 1080 and 1576 approx 1300
       (i) Between 1741 and 1825 approx 1800
       (j) Between 1952 and present

Unit 31

1 (a) The lady's name is Jane Smith (library ticket)
   (b) She enjoys reading (library ticket)
   (c) She gets her books from Putney library (library ticket)
   (d) She has a joint account at Pitmans bank and her husband's name is Paul (cheque book)
   (e) She enjoys classical music – (ticket to Beethoven concert at the Royal Albert Hall)
   (f) She has use of a Ford car – car keys
   (g) She enjoys eating peppermints
   (h) She is a 'weight watcher' because she uses sweeteners rather than sugar
   (i) She is a mother because she has a child allowance book in her name; if you looked inside you would find out the children's names.
   (j) She is a member of or interested in the WI
2 You could return the bag by using the address on the child allowance book
3 There is a footprint of a dog, therefore, the Romans kept dogs
4 The dates, and so the order you would have found them would be:

Elizabeth II	not before 1952
George V	not before 1910 (1910 – 1936)
Victoria	not before 1837 (1837 – 1901)
William IV	not before 1830 (1830 – 1837)
George III	not before 1760 (1760 – 1820)
George II	not before 1727 (1727 – 1760)
Anne	not before 1702 (1702 – 1714)
James II	not before 1685 (1685 – 1688)
Charles I	not before 1625 (1625 – 1649)
Elizabeth I	not before 1558 (1558 – 1603)
Edward VI	not before 1547 (1547 – 1553)
Henry VII	not before 1485 (1485 – 1509)

Unit 32

1 Primary
2 Primary
3 Secondary
4 Secondary
5 Secondary
6 Primary

Unit 33

1 942.073
2 942.033
3 391
4 391
5 932
6 937
7 942
8 942.02
9 942.021
10 942.05
11 942.0111
12 942.02
13 940.1
14 941.081
15 942.07
16 728.8

Unit 34

The Spanish Armada, J. Smith
Phillip II of Spain 1527 – 1598, G. Perez
The Duke of Medina Sidonia, T. Fleming
The Spanish Armada, P. Sanchez
Sir Frances Drake, his life and times, D. Raleigh
The Elizabethan Age, P. Knutt
The Sea-dogs of Elizabethan times, C. Hoarse

Unit 35
Text page 115:

Revision unit Newspapers
1. Bar room
2. White Hart Hotel, Caversham, Reading
3. Low, on south side of building, detached
4. Large fire
5. Inspector May G.W.R.
6. Told (Apprised) the inmates
7. Reading Volunteer Fire Brigade
8. Anything that can be carried
9. Palmer
10. Mr Rawstone
11. They fixed a standpipe
12. Steam fire engine
13. The river
14. Gate leading down to river
15. Old and contained inflammable spirits
16. 3.30 p.m.
17. Maiden Erlegh Fire Brigade
18. Speed, quickness
19. A defective flue
20. Corporation of Reading
21. A.G. Bona
22. London and Lancashire office
23. Bar, three ground floor rooms and contents burned out. Roof off – Four rooms in basement and contents severely damaged by fire, heat, smoke and water
24. Fire, heat, smoke and water
25. Read official report

Glossary

A fuller definition of the following words may be found in a dictionary.

amalgamated mixed or joined.
ancestor a person from whom your father or mother is descended.
archives public records. Place in which these records are kept.
archivist a keeper of archives.
barter exchange of articles for something similar or something required – swapping.
chronological arrangement of events according to the time they took place.
compiled collected.
confidential spoken or written in secret. Only to be read or heard by those entrusted to keep the secret.
deduction using available information to make a guess as to the possible answer to a question or theory.
delicate frail.
discriminate to observe the differences between, or make a distinction between two or more things.
environment surroundings.
established set up, founded.
evident obvious to mind and eyes. Clear, plain.
extract (noun) a copied passage from a book etc; (verb) to take out.
facade the face of a building.
hoard to store, sometimes secretly.
interpret to work out the meaning of something.

malformed faulty.
military to do with the army.
minster church or a monastery. Any large church.
political to do with the government or politics.
pressgang a group of armed men who kidnapped able-bodied men from inns and public houses to serve in the Royal Navy of the 18th century.
proficient expert.
propaganda organized scheme to influence people to believe some fact.
public school a fee-paying school where, usually, the pupils are boarders.
relevant having a bearing on.
relic something surviving from the past.
research discovery of facts by a course of investigation.
restrictions limitations.
scan to read very quickly.
sensationalize to make exciting or to exaggerate.
sequence order of things. Succession.
significance meaning, importance.
source origin of document or work etc, providing evidence to support theory or investigation.
specific definite, precise.
substantiate to give substance to, to bring evidence for, to establish the truth of.
summarize to sum up. Make a brief description taking out needless detail.
superficial on the surface, not deep.